First World War
and Army of Occupation
War Diary
France, Belgium and Germany

18 DIVISION
Divisional Troops
83 Brigade Royal Field Artillery
24 July 1915 - 29 July 1919

WO95/2025/1

The Naval & Military Press Ltd
www.nmarchive.com
Published in association with The National Archives

Published by

The Naval & Military Press Ltd

Unit 10 Ridgewood Industrial Park,

Uckfield, East Sussex,

TN22 5QE England

Tel: +44 (0) 1825 749494

www.naval-military-press.com

www.nmarchive.com

This diary has been reprinted in facsimile from the original. Any imperfections are inevitably reproduced and the quality may fall short of modern type and cartographic standards.

© Crown Copyright
Images reproduced by permission of The National Archives, London, England, 2015.

Contents

Document type	Place/Title	Date From	Date To
Heading	WO95/2025 18 Division Divisional Troops 83 Brigade Royal Filed Artillery Jul 1915-Jul 1919		
Heading	18th Division 83rd Brigade R.F.A. Jly 1915-Mar 1919		
Heading	War Diary 83rd Brigade R.F.A.		
Heading	18th Division 83rd Brigade R.F.A. Vol. I From 24 Jly to 31 aug 15		
War Diary	Heytesbury	24/07/1915	24/07/1915
War Diary	Southampton	25/07/1915	25/07/1915
War Diary	Harve	26/07/1915	27/07/1915
War Diary	Longueau	27/07/1915	27/07/1915
War Diary	Naours	28/07/1915	29/07/1915
War Diary	Mericourt	30/07/1915	04/08/1915
War Diary	Bellevue	05/08/1915	31/08/1915
Miscellaneous	Appendix I	21/08/1915	21/08/1915
Heading	18th Division 83rd Brigade R.F.A. Vol. 2 Sept 15		
War Diary	Bellevue	01/09/1915	30/09/1915
Diagram etc			
Heading	18th Division 83rd Bde. R79 Vol. 3 Oct 15		
War Diary	Bellevue	01/10/1915	31/10/1915
Heading	18th Division 83rd Bde. R.F.A. Vol 4 Nov 15		
War Diary	Bellvue	01/11/1915	30/11/1915
Heading	18th Div 83rd Bde Rfa Vol 5		
War Diary	Bellvue	01/12/1915	31/12/1915
Heading	83rd Bde R. Fa Vol: 6 Jan		
War Diary	Bellvue	01/01/1916	11/01/1916
War Diary	Bellvue Farm	12/01/1916	29/02/1916
Heading	83rd FA Vol 8		
War Diary	Bellvue Farm	01/03/1916	21/03/1916
War Diary	Bray	22/03/1916	07/05/1916
War Diary	Argoeuves	17/05/1916	26/05/1916
War Diary	Maricourt Valley	28/05/1916	31/05/1916
War Diary	Suzanne	01/05/1916	31/05/1916
War Diary	Arcoeuves	01/06/1916	19/06/1916
War Diary	Billon Wood	19/06/1916	30/06/1916
Heading	83rd Bde. R.F.A. Vol 12		
War Diary	Billon Wood	01/07/1916	07/07/1916
War Diary	Carnoy	08/07/1916	14/07/1916
War Diary	The Twins	15/07/1916	22/07/1916
War Diary	Fontaine Sur. Somme	23/07/1916	27/07/1916
War Diary	Caestre	28/07/1916	31/07/1916
Operation(al) Order(s)	Operation Order No. 1 by Brigadier General S.F. Metcalfe. D.S.O. Comdg. Arty. 18th Divn	19/06/1916	19/06/1916
Miscellaneous	Programme of Preliminary Bombardment. Appendix "A"		
Miscellaneous	Bombardment To Support Assault Appendix "B"		
Miscellaneous	No. 2 Amendments to 18th Divnl. Arty. Operation Order No. 1.	27/06/1916	27/06/1916
Miscellaneous	Appendix "C" Approximate Allotment of Ammunition For Various Tasks		
Miscellaneous	Appendix "D" Preparations For Forward Advance.		

Miscellaneous	Reference Artillery Lifts Shown by Coloured Lines		
Map	XV Corps		
Map	Forward Routes To Be Opened		
Miscellaneous	Amendments To 18th Divisional Artillery Order No. 1	24/06/1916	24/06/1916
Operation(al) Order(s)	18th Divisional Artillery Operation Order No. 3 by Brigadier General S.F. Metcalfe, D.S.O.	06/07/1916	06/07/1916
Operation(al) Order(s)	18th Div. Art. Operation Order No. 2	06/07/1916	06/07/1916
Operation(al) Order(s)	3rd Div. Arty. O.O. No. 6	13/07/1916	13/07/1916
Miscellaneous	Explanation of Attached Time Table.		
Miscellaneous	Time Table	13/07/1916	13/07/1916
Map	Position of Wire Taken From Aeroplane Photographs	05/07/1916	05/07/1916
Miscellaneous	Jane	24/07/1916	24/07/1916
Miscellaneous	Move of 18th Division (Artillery)	24/07/1916	24/07/1916
Miscellaneous	Time Table Longpre Station		
Operation(al) Order(s)	18th Division Artillery Order No. 5 by Brigadier General S.F. Metcalfe, D.S.O.	25/07/1916	25/07/1916
War Diary	Caestre	01/08/1916	03/08/1916
War Diary	Armentieres	04/08/1916	25/08/1916
War Diary	Croix Du Bac	26/08/1916	31/08/1916
War Diary	Albert	01/09/1916	01/09/1916
War Diary	Near Contalmaison	02/09/1916	30/09/1916
Heading	War Diary For October 1916 83rd Bde R.F.A. Vol 15		
War Diary	Near Aveluy	01/10/1916	09/10/1916
War Diary	Authville Wood	09/10/1916	31/10/1916
Heading	War Diary For November 1916 83rd Bde R.F.A. Vol 16		
War Diary		01/11/1916	30/11/1916
Heading	War Diary of 83rd Brigade R.F.A. From December 1st 1916 to December 31st 1916 Volume VI		
War Diary		01/12/1916	31/01/1917
Heading	83rd Bde R.F.A. Feb Vol XIX		
Heading	83rd Brigade R.F.A. Vol 19		
War Diary		01/02/1917	28/02/1917
Heading	War Diary For March 1917 83rd Brigade R.F.A. 18th Divisional Artillery Vol 20		
War Diary		01/03/1917	18/03/1917
War Diary	Irles	19/03/1917	31/03/1917
Heading	War Diary For April 1917 83rd Brigade R.F.A. Vol 21		
War Diary		01/04/1917	30/04/1917
Heading	Vol 22 War Diary For May 1917 83rd Brigade R.F.A.		
War Diary	Heninel	01/05/1917	24/05/1917
War Diary	Cojeul Valley	25/05/1917	31/05/1917
Heading	83rd Bde. R.F.A. June 1917 Vol 23		
War Diary		01/06/1917	30/06/1917
War Diary	Dickebusch	01/08/1917	30/09/1917
Heading	18th Divisional Artillery. 83rd Brigade, R.F.A. War Diary For Month of October, 1917		
War Diary	St Julien Area	01/10/1917	31/10/1917
War Diary		01/11/1917	02/02/1918
War Diary	Hamhoek	03/02/1918	11/02/1918
War Diary	Porqueri-Court	12/02/1918	14/02/1918
War Diary	Guiscard	15/02/1918	28/02/1918
Heading	18th Div. War Diary Headquarters, 83rd Brigade, R.F.A. March 1918		
War Diary		01/03/1918	13/04/1918

Heading	18th Div. Headquarters. 83rd Brigade, R.F.A. April 1918		
War Diary		01/04/1918	31/07/1918
Heading	18th Division Artillery 83rd Brigade Royal Field Artillery August 1918		
War Diary	Field	01/08/1918	07/08/1918
War Diary	Mericourt L'Abbee	08/08/1918	10/08/1918
War Diary	Morlancourt	11/08/1918	24/08/1918
War Diary	Meaulte	25/08/1918	25/08/1918
War Diary	Albert	26/08/1918	26/08/1918
War Diary	Fricourt	27/08/1918	27/08/1918
War Diary	Montauban	28/08/1918	29/08/1918
War Diary	Guillemont	30/08/1918	31/08/1918
War Diary		01/09/1918	30/09/1918
War Diary	Field	01/10/1918	05/10/1918
War Diary	France	05/10/1918	30/11/1918
War Diary	Field	01/12/1918	30/01/1919
War Diary	Reumont	01/02/1919	13/02/1919
Heading	D.A.A.G. (I) Herewith War Diary of 83rd Bde R.F.A. for the Month of March 1919		
War Diary	Montigny	14/03/1919	29/07/1919

WO 95/2025

① 18 Division
Divisional Troops

83 Brigade Royal Field Artillery

Jul 1915 – Jul 1919.

18TH DIVISION

83RD BRIGADE R.F.A.
JLY 1915 - MAR 1919

18.D Arty

War Diary

83rd Brigade R.F.A.

121/6099

18ᵗʰ Division

83ʳᵈ Brigade R.F.A.
Vol. I

From 24 July to 31 Aug. 15

Nov 19

Army Form C. 2118

WAR DIARY
or
INTELLIGENCE SUMMARY

(Erase heading not required.)

Instructions regarding War Diaries and Intelligence Summaries are contained in F.S. Regs., Part II. and the Staff Manual respectively. Title Pages will be prepared in manuscript.

Place	Date	Hour	Summary of Events and Information	Remarks and references to Appendices
Heytesbury	24/9/15		The 83rd Bde R.F.A. entrained at Codford and Warminster for Southampton A, B, BAC and Bde Hd Qrs from Codford, C and D from Warminster. First unit started at 6.30 p.m. and last unit at 3.20 a.m. 25.9.15 all arrangements went very smoothly	
Southampton	25/9/15	4 p.m.	First steamer "Rossetti" sailed at 4 p.m. with Hd Qrs, A and B Batteries. Other units left in succession	
Havre	26/9/15		Arrived Havre and after disembarkation, Hd Qrs, A and D Btys marched to No 5 camp. B and C Batteries remained in Havre until time for entraining. Issues were made out for stores required to complete to establishment and a few articles drawn but units are still deficient of several articles, principally spare parts for guns.	
		11.30 a.m.	Hd Qrs and A Bty entrained	
	27/9/15	2.30 a.m.	D. Bty entrained.	
Longueau		12.45 p.m.	Hd Qrs and A Bty arrived and disentrained. Orders received to march to NAOURS.	
		5.30 p.m.	Arrived at NAOURS and found B and C Batteries had arrived earlier. D Bty and DAC arrived later. Guns and wagons were parked in woods and orchards and horses tied to lines stabled between vehicles. All hid well from aircraft observation. Received orders that Bde was to join 57th Div., Col Hardiffe arranged with O.i.c Batteries to meet him at 8.30 a.m. 28th to reconnoitre	

WAR DIARY
or
INTELLIGENCE SUMMARY
(Erase heading not required.)

Army Form C. 2118

Place	Date	Hour	Summary of Events and Information	Remarks and references to Appendices
NAOURS	28/7/15		Lee Metcalfe and O.C. Batteries started for ALBERT to visit French lines and see position to be taken over.	
—	29/7/15	6 a.m.	Orders received to march 29th to MERICOURT. Brigade marched off. D Battery leading followed by A.B.C. The B.A.C. were ordered to remain at MERICOURT under orders of C.O.C. R.A. 151st Div. Brigade marched through TALMAS, GUERRIEUX, RIBEMONT to MERICOURT. First Battery arrived, followed at about ½ hour intervals by the others.	
MERICOURT		2 p.m.		
—	30/7/15		Orders received that D/Sh was to be sent to the Highland Brigade and only 3 Batteries left in Brigade. Colonel and O.C. Batteries (Batteries) again went out to reconnoitre position. D Battery Gunners were taken out to prepare gun pits. Two guns of D were taken out and placed in position. One gun each from A, B and C taken out and put in French gun pits. Points were registered for each Battery.	
—	1/8/15		Batteries again registered until one gun acal.	
—	2/8/15		Nothing to report	
—	3/8/15		Remaining section of D taken out to position near BOUZINCOURT. B.A.C. arrived at MERICOURT	
—	4/8/15	6.30 p.m.	Brigade marched to Farm BELLEVUE. French gun taken out of pits and left our in the open covered with tarpaulin. Our gun put into position	

Army Form C. 2118

WAR DIARY
or
INTELLIGENCE SUMMARY
(Erase heading not required.)

Instructions regarding War Diaries and Intelligence Summaries are contained in F.S. Regs., Part II. and the Staff Manual respectively. Title Pages will be prepared in manuscript.

Place	Date	Hour	Summary of Events and Information	Remarks and references to Appendices
BELLEVUE	5/8/15		Batteries completed registration of Zones	
		8 p.m.	French Batteries marched away.	
			During night several explosions from trench mortars were heard	
	6/8/15	4.30 P.M.	Enemy shelled ALBERT. About 5 to 10 rounds dropped in the town and one near B Battery position.	
			Brigade was ordered to take further trenches on our right into our Zone. These were allotted to A. Bty. Battery registered new points. C Battery's Zone altered owing to change in A Zone. C registered new points	
	7/8/15		Nothing to report except that B.A.C. marched to BUIRE	
	8/8/15	5 p.m.	B. Battery requested by Infantry to open fire on trench mortar. This was done.	
		11.15 p.m.	B Battery again requested to open fire on enemy trenches. Colonel rang up 57th Div R.A. and asked for Howitzer fire. Two rounds were fired but owing to smoke and dust caused by the explosion of two minenwerfer were not observed. Part of our Inf trenches were blown in and several men buried.	
			Infantry requested B Battery to open heavy fire on enemy as soon as it became light to enable them to repair damage to their trenches.	
			A few shells fell into ALBERT and two near B Battery position	
	9/8/15		Nothing to report	

Army Form C. 2118

WAR DIARY
or
INTELLIGENCE SUMMARY
(Erase heading not required.)

Instructions regarding War Diaries and Intelligence Summaries are contained in F.S. Regs., Part II. and the Staff Manual respectively. Title Pages will be prepared in manuscript.

Place	Date	Hour	Summary of Events and Information	Remarks and references to Appendices
BELLEVUE	10/8/15		Nothing to report	
—	11/8/15	9 p.m	O.C. D. Bty reports a gun burst while firing, muzzle end of piece blown off. No casualties	
—	12/8/15		Nothing to report	
—	13/8/15		About 10.30 am Engineers blew up mound under Cannon Street. B and C Batteries fired 12 and 13 rounds respectively at locality. Reported that only a few sand bags were dislodged on Trenches and mine mouth entirely uncertain direction of Enemy.	
—		2.30 pm	Enemy shelled ALBERT and locality of Hill 106 and Crest above B Battery position. Telephone wire attached to French heavy Battery and wireless station established the far for the purpose of communicating with our craft	
—	14/8/15	4 pm	Guns which bombed ALBERT are thought to be near CONTALMAISON and A Battery fired. No observation possible	
—	15/8/15		One howitzer battery placed under orders of Bde Commander from 17 inst. Wire laid to their position	
—		11.30 a.m	Enemy machine gun position located by C. Bty. 13 rounds fired at request of Infantry at machine gun position. Observed to be effective	
—	16/8/15		D Bty report having received near gun to rifles damaged on	
—	—	4 pm	LA BOISELLE bombarded by 6" and 5" Howitzers, 18 and 15 pr guns. 6" Howitzers opened, 18 and 15 pr Batteries fired 4 rds each after, 6". 5" How then fired 10 rds. 3 min pause after which gun batteries fired 4 rds each. 6" How then fired 6 rds and field Batteries followed with 4 rounds each	

1875 Wt. W593/826 1,000,000 4/15 J.B.C. & A. A.D.S.S./Forms/C. 2118.

WAR DIARY or INTELLIGENCE SUMMARY

Army Form C. 2118

Place	Date	Hour	Summary of Events and Information	Remarks and references to Appendices
BELLUE	17.8.15.	11.45 am	A Battery registered position of enemy machine gun in forward sap from L64	
		5 p.m.	About 12 rds from enemy field gun fell on HILL 106	
		6.50 p.m.	9 rounds from enemy field gun fell in ALBERT	
	18.8.15	5.15 p.m.	Lieut Logan and two gunners D Bty proceeded to St OMER to give evidence on Court of Inquiry on Lewis gun	
		10 —	D Battery shelled working party and trench mortar	
		9.55 —	A Bty fired 3 rds at same target	
		10.5 —	A Bty shelled working party at 464. 4 rounds. Work stopped	
		3.15 —	461. 4 — — —	
		5 h —	C — — — — —	
			Enemy shelled HILL 106 and dropped a few shells near crest in front of D.Bty position	
	19.8.15	7.30 a.m.	Mine was exploded under enemy trench at 452. B Battery fired 30 rounds at La BOISELLE immediately after explosion. Was reported successful	
		10.15 — and 2.15 am	D Battery fired at German transport on road	
			working parties at points 464, 475 + 443 were shelled and work stopped	
		4h— 7.45h—	Enemy shelled wood on crest in front of D position and own infantry trenches	
		7h—	Enemy Rifleman fired on by anti air craft gun	
	20.8.15		Batteries fired at new trench and machine gun emplacements at 475, 462 and La BOISELLE	
			Enemy field gun fired at road near HILL 106 and ridge running N from that point. 10 rounds	
	21.8.15	6 p.m and 7.30 h —	Batteries fired at working parties at 462, 464, 475. C.105 verified knowledge line	
			Enemy shelled ALBERT	

WAR DIARY
or
INTELLIGENCE SUMMARY

(Erase heading not required.)

Army Form C. 2118

Instructions regarding War Diaries and Intelligence Summaries are contained in F.S. Regs., Part II. and the Staff Manual respectively. Title Pages will be prepared in manuscript.

Place	Date	Hour	Summary of Events and Information	Remarks and references to Appendices
BELLEVUE	22.8.15		Batteries fired on CONTALMAISON and working parties at 464, 475, 462 and transport on road near 439. Enemy fired 3 rounds into ALBERT at 7.15 p.m. Two enemy aeroplanes passed over our position during evening of 22nd and morning of 23rd. They was fired on by anti aircraft gun.	Appendix I
"	23.8.15	9.20 a.m. to 10.15 a.m.	Enemy fired 23 rounds from Y.Y gun at C.135 position. No gun pit or shelter actually hit. During take point to gun being near 7791 on 76B9. Range about 5470 yds. During the day and night Batteries fired at working parties on 464, 475, 443 and trench mortars in 443. Working parties and mortars stopped.	
"	24.8.15	7.25 a.m.	Enemy aeroplane passed from S. turned E. and then circled away to N. fired on by A.A gun. Four Officers joined for attachment. One each was sent to A, B, C & D Btys. Batteries fired during day and night at Trench Mortars, machine gun emplacements and working parties or request of Infantry. Working parties ceased. Enemy shelled a wood in front of B Battery position continuously from 4 p.m. also 8 p.m. and occasionally during the night.	
"	25.8.15		Nothing to report	
"	26.8.15		—	
"	27.8.15	8.5 p.m. to 9.45 p.m.	Batteries fired on trench mortars and working parties at 475 and 462 and at enemy transport near CONTALMAISON. Mortars and working parties ceased and no further sounds of transport heard. Enemy shelled wood in front of B Battery position heavily between 11.30 p.m. and 1 a.m. 28th. Junction opposite 43 b shelled by enemy field guns. 3 rounds from D.35 position in the direction of FERME DU MOUVET.	
"	28/8/15		Aeroplane unidentified flew over BELLEVUE from direction of CARNOY & BOUZINCOURT	

WAR DIARY or INTELLIGENCE SUMMARY

Army Form C. 2118

Place	Date	Hour	Summary of Events and Information	Remarks and references to Appendices
BELLEVUE	28.8.15		Batteries fired at working parties at 462 and 475 and at transport on road near CONTALMAISON. Working ceased and no further rounds of transport heard. O.C. 152nd Bde decided to repair trenches which had been damaged by enemy mines. Arrangements were made that work always stopped at down (3.30 a.m.) 29th at which time balloon were prepared to open fire on any trench mortars, machine gun or battalion that opened fire on our working parties. 6" Howitzer, 5" Howitzer and 15pr Batteries were also ready in readiness. The work progressed all day without any serious hindrances, the gun firing only a few occasional shots at trench mortars. Enemy shelled roads in front of B and C position and ALBERT.	
" "	29.8.15		Same arrangement as before were made to safeguard infantry parties repairing trenches, at 4–25 a.m. enemy trench mortars became active and B. Battery fired 30 rounds and 5" Howitzer 25 rds at which silenced them. Work on trench proceeded.	
" "	30.8.15 12.30 p.m.		Working parties at 475 and transport near CONTALMAISON fired at. Enemy Battery fired 16 rounds into D Battery position. Shells were 10.15 c.m. Howitzer, range about 4,525 yds and from bearing taken, position of gun is approximately 427. Shelling continued painted red, west of east arm to which and one measuring driving band and a day later up into very small pieces. What was apparently an enemy post was seen opposite a reference on 3rd m. the enemy gun positions were shelled by D B4 and 5" Howitzer Batteries action at 2.30 p.m. at 427 and 428. or 2.30 p.m also had been removed. B and C Batteries shelled trench mortars and machine gun emplacements at 456, 457 and 462. Gun fire from machine gun stopped.	
" "	31.8.15		A and C Batteries registered targets by aid of aeroplane observation. Enemy shelled HILL 106 and ALBERT – BÉCOURT road.	

Rudeaux
Lt Col R.F.A.
Comdg 83rd Brigade R.F.A.

Appendix I

O. 8.30 p.m.

The C.R.A. is glad to forward the following
copy of correspondence which shows that
the "entente" with the infantry has been
well established and reflects great credit
on the O.R. F. & S.D.
22.8.15.   Midgeme Brig Gen 51st Div

*   *   *

HdQrs. 153 Inf Bde
On relief from Sector No.3 I should like to
bring to notice the very effective & practical
assistance rendered to the infantry
by the artillery on this sector, with the
result that a mutual confidence and
co-operation has been established between
the two arms.

The OC "B" Battery, responsible for this
sector, has spared no pains, either by
day or night to assist infantry officers
in identifying points where hostile
trench mortars or machine guns have
been detected, and whenever fire has been
asked for it has been effectively rendered
within a few minutes.
                    Sd/ H.S. Allen Lt Col
21.8.15.   Comdg 1/7 R.H.

HdQrs 51st Div.
It gives me great pleasure to forward the
attached message from Officer i/c Black
Watch. I am sure the Commanding Officers of the
other Battalions in this Brigade can say the
same thing. I have personally observed

12/7051

18th Division

83rd Brigade R.F.A.
Vol: 2.
Sept. 15

WAR DIARY or INTELLIGENCE SUMMARY

Army Form C. 2118

83rd Bde R.F.A.

Place	Date	Hour	Summary of Events and Information	Remarks and references to Appendices
BELLEVUE	1.9.15		Nothing to report	
"	2.9.15		Batteries fired at working parties at 464, 475 and 477	
		4.30 pm	Enemy shelled ALBERT.	
"	3.9.15		Batteries fired at working parties and enemy again shelled ALBERT and vicinity. Orders received about D Battery would be relieved in 57th Div line by a Battery of 2nd High Dec D/Battery to rejoin 18 Div and be billeted at BONNAY. One and one B.A.C. to be taken on strength of 18 Div	
"	4.9.15		Batteries shelled working parties at 464 & 475 and shoes and vehicle near point 7586	
"	5.9.15		Enemy aeroplane brought down by Aerial Aeroplanes. Reported to have fallen near LA BOISSELLE	
"	6.9.15		Nothing to report	
"	7.9.15		Batteries shelled working parties at 443 and 475	
"	8.9.15		Batteries shelled working parties and machine gun emplacements at 457, 459, 463 and 477	
"	9.9.15		Enemy aeroplane flew over Battery position and branches.	
"	10.9.15		Batteries fired at working parties at 454 and 459 and French mortar near 462 Enemy gun shelled MEAULTE — BECOURT Road E of ALBERT near Nothill was fired from LA BOISSELLE @ 8 pm and another from a point 500 yds S of LA BOISSELLE. Much aircraft and an many round 464 - 475.	
"	11.9.15		Working parties and trench mortars shelled by A.B.C. Btys	
"	12.9.15		Batteries shelled CONTALMAISON and working parties at 443, 475 and 477. Enemy shelled ALBERT - BECOURT road and ALBERT. The latter with 5.9 shells one of which was found unexploded.	
"	13.9.15		Batteries shelled 476, 452 and 454 in retaliation, at working parties and trench mortars fire observed effective. Enemy shelled Renfrew (How) Battery (6.15 pm). Enemy aeroplane passed over 3 times during early morning and afternoon	

Army Form C. 2118

83rd Bde RFA

WAR DIARY
or
INTELLIGENCE SUMMARY
(Erase heading not required.)

Instructions regarding War Diaries and Intelligence Summaries are contained in F. S. Regs., Part II. and the Staff Manual respectively. Title Pages will be prepared in manuscript.

Place	Date	Hour	Summary of Events and Information	Remarks and references to Appendices
BELLEVUE	14.9.15			
	15.9.15		Batteries fired at working parties @ 475 and NE corner of LA BOISSELLE. Verbal orders received that Bdes would revert to 18 Div on 18th inst. D Bty would come under orders of Lt Metcalfe, and that the 1Bde with A Bty 55th Bde arrived form the left group 15 Div and Zone would be Sections E.2. and E.3.	
	16.9.15		'A' Bty fired 14 rounds as a wire cutting experiment, a channel about 6 feet wide was cut through entanglements near 477. Range about 3500 yards. Enemy shelled road over Hill 106 and ALBERT. Batteries fired at working parties at 443, Observation station Rafer of Church at LA BOISSELLE and trench mortar near 462. Enemy shelled ALBERT and infantry/trenches. On action A Bty relieved by one section B/84 DE TALLE A moved to wagon lines, D Battery moved into wagon line from BOIS . One man of D missed through asphyxia of fumes the pistons mp. after previous was shelled. One man wounded by rifle fire. Position selected for A and D Batteries and for A/85 and preparation for occupation started.	
	17.9.15		Batteries will move to new position A. K.36.6.3 B.0.6.2.8 C. K.36.6.6. D K.36.7.7 a/85 K 36. 2. 7. Remaining section of A Bty relieved by B/84. Brigade Wagon lines moved to a position near K.14. 154, just S W of ALBERT and near ALBERT – ROUEN road. Batteries fired at enemy trenches and trench mortar near 462	
	18.9.15		nothing to report	
	19.9.15		Batteries shelled working parties at 443 and 462 Enemy shelled B/84 position just E of FARM BELLEVUE during afternoon with 5"9 shell Two enemy batteries located at points 6667 and 6956	
	20.9.15		Batteries shelled transport on road near LA BOISSELLE, trench mortars near 462 and enemy trenches in retaliation Enemy shelled PAR M BELLEVUE from 11 a.m. to 1.45 p.m. Several enemy aeroplanes flew over battery positions during the day	

1875. Wt. W593/826 1,000,000 4/15 J.B.C. & A. A.D.S.S./Forms/C. 2118.

WAR DIARY
INTELLIGENCE SUMMARY
(Erase heading not required.)

83rd Bde R.F.A.

Army Form C. 2118

Place	Date	Hour	Summary of Events and Information	Remarks and references to Appendices
BELLEVUE	21.9.15		Batteries fired several tests and also at enemy trenches in retaliation at 7 a.m., 7.35 a.m. and noon, enemy aeroplane flew over	
—	22.9.15		Batteries fired at working parties and trench mortar near 462. Enemy shelled ALBERT from 12.30 p.m. to 5.30 p.m. Enemy aeroplanes again very active.	
—	23.9.15		Batteries fired at working parties and during the afternoon B and C Batteries fired 168 rounds at wire entanglements. a few shots from enemy field gun fell on HILL 106	
—	24.9.15		Batteries registered south between 465 and 477 and trench mortar positions near 459	
—	25.9.15		Batteries again registered and bombarded wire entanglements. Enemy fired a few shell into ALBERT	
—		6.45 p.m.	Enemy sent up several red and white flares and then opened heavy machine gun fire on our trenches. B and C Batteries fired at various points in enemy trenches and reg registered.	
—	26.9.15		Enemy shelled HILL 106 with light field gun	
—	27.9.15		Enemy fired a few shell at used road going over HILL 106	
—	28.9.15		Enemy fired a few shell at B.Dy position and FARM BELLEVUE	
—	29.9.15		Nothing to report	
—	30.9.15		Enemy shelled HILL 106. Enemy aeroplanes passed over several times during morning	

Metcalfe
Lieut Col R.F.A
Comdg 83rd Bde R.F.A

121/7593

18th Kwann

63 Shde: R7a.
fol: 3

Oct 15

Army Form C. 2118

WAR DIARY
or
INTELLIGENCE SUMMARY 83rd Bde R.F.A

(Erase heading not required.)

Instructions regarding War Diaries and Intelligence Summaries are contained in F. S. Regs., Part II. and the Staff Manual respectively. Title Pages will be prepared in manuscript.

Place	Date	Hour	Summary of Events and Information	Remarks and references to Appendices
BELLEVUE	1.10.15		Batteries fired at various targets in retaliation	
		7.30 a.m	Enemy shelled ALBERT and HILL 106. Enemy aeroplane flew over battery positions	
"	2.10.15		Enemy shelled ALBERT and HILL 106	
"	3.10.15		Batteries fired at working parties at X 20 a 4. 6. Enemy shelled ALBERT and HILL 106	
"	4.10.15		Enemy shelled ALBERT and HILL 106. Brigade formed 5.10.14	
"	5.10.15		Nothing to report.	
"	6.10.15		Nothing to report	
"	7.10.15		Batteries fired at LA BOISSELLE in retaliation. Enemy shelled HILL 106	
"	8.10.15		Enemy shelled ALBERT from 10h a.m. to 12 a.m.	
"	9.10.15		Nothing to report	
"	10.10.15		Enemy shelled HILL 106. Enemy aeroplanes active.	
"	11.10.15		"A" Battery registered reverse fronts in LA BOISSELLE. Enemy first 6 rounds at FARM BELLEVUE. Enemy aeroplanes active	
"	12.10.15		"A" and "D" Batteries registered point at X 26 D 7 7, X 14 a 6. 7 and X 8 d 5. 3. Enemy shelled HILL 106	
"	13.10.15		"A" Battery registered and "C" 136. fired in retaliation	
"	14.10.15		"A" and "D" Batteries registered and "C" 136 fired in retaliation. Enemy shelled HILL 106 and BAPUME Rd. Enemy aeroplanes flew over at 4-30 h.m. flying towards POZIERS	
"	15.10.15		Nothing to report	

WAR DIARY

INTELLIGENCE SUMMARY — 83rd Bde R.F.A.

Army Form C. 2118

(Erase heading not required.)

Instructions regarding War Diaries and Intelligence Summaries are contained in F.S. Regs., Part II. and the Staff Manual respectively. Title Pages will be prepared in manuscript.

Place	Date	Hour	Summary of Events and Information	Remarks and references to Appendices
BELLEVUE	16.10.15		'A' and 'D' Batteries registered points at X 21 C 7.9 and LA BOISELLE, 'B' and 'C' Batteries fired at working parties and trenches after explosion of mine near IL OT	
"	17.10.15		A,B,C and D Batteries fired at working parties and in retaliation. Enemy shelled Hill 106, C Bty position and ALBERT	
"	18.10.15		Nothing to report	
"	19.10.15		Batteries shelled LA BOISELLE in retaliation. Enemy shelled our trenches	
"	20.10.15		Enemy shelled ALBERT. Shells fell near position of 'C' Bty wagon line. Batteries fired in retaliation	
"	21.10.15		Batteries fired at working parties in LA BOISELLE. Enemy shelled ALBERT	
"	22.10.15		Batteries fired at working parties and registered points on BOISELLE – POZIERES Rd and at machine gun emplacements. Enemy aeroplane flew over position	
"	23.10.15		Batteries fired at working parties and at transport on CONTALMAISON Rd and registered C and D aeroplane observation. Enemy shelled Hill 106	
"	24.10.15		Enemy aeroplanes active. Nothing to report	
"	25.10.15		Enemy shelled ALBERT	
"	26.10.15		Batteries fired in retaliation at enemy trenches and observing stations. Enemy shelled vicinity of position from 11 a.m. to noon. 1 man of B. Bty wounded	
"	27.10.15		Batteries fired in retaliation at enemy trenches. Enemy fired a few rounds at BOIS NOIR	

WAR DIARY or INTELLIGENCE SUMMARY

Army Form C. 2118

83rd Bde R.F.a

Place	Date	Hour	Summary of Events and Information	Remarks and references to Appendices
BELLVUE	28/10/15		"D" and "B" Batteries fires at working parties in LAB 1163446 and 58x15 PBS. Enemy shelled neighbourhood of BECOURT	
-"-	29/10/15		Batteries fires on LABOISSELLE in retaliation to trench mortar fire. Enemy shelled "C" Bty wagon lines with five rounds	
-"-	30/10/15		Batteries fires on LA BOISSELLE in retaliation to trench mortar fire. "C" Bty fires on working party. Enemy shelled Bois No.18.	
-"-	31/10/15		"A" Bty registered various points. Enemy shelled ALBERT	

Clyde Crew R.a
Adjutant
for Lieut. Colonel
Com'dg 83rd Brigade Royal Field Artillery

83 Bar: R.2a.
Vol: 4

12/1795

18th Kværn

Nov. 15

Army Form C. 2118

WAR DIARY
or
INTELLIGENCE SUMMARY

(Erase heading not required.)

Instructions regarding War Diaries and Intelligence Summaries are contained in F.S. Regs., Part II. and the Staff Manual respectively. Title Pages will be prepared in manuscript.

Place	Date	Hour	Summary of Events and Information	Remarks and references to Appendices
BELLVUE	1/11/15		"A" Battery fired at working Party. Battries bombarded LA BOISSELLE in Retaliation to Senet Morton fire.	
— "" —	2/11/15		Enemy shelled BECOURT and BECORDEL	
— "" —	3/11/15		"C" and "D" shelled Enemy fire trenches in retaliation to Senet Morters. Enemy shelled Bois Noir	
— "" —	4/11/15		"B" Bty fired 4 rounds into LA BOISSELLE. "D" Bty fired 3 rounds at Senet Morter at pt X14 c4.5.15	
— "" —			Enemy fired 3 rounds which fell on Road over Hill 106.	
— "" —	5/11/15		"C" Bty shelled fire trench in X20A with 4 rounds in retaliation	
— "" —			Enemy shelled "C" Bty position and road over HILL 106.	
— "" —			"B" Battery fired at working party. "C" Bty fired on enemy trenches in retaliation. Enemy shelled ALBERT and road over Hill 106	
— "" —	6/11/15		"A" and "B" Battries registered points in LA BOISSELLE. "B" Bty fired at working Party	
— "" —	7/11/15		"D" Bty fired at Sniper post. "B" Bty fired 13 rounds in LA BOISELLE in retaliation.	
— "" —	8/11/15		Enemy aeroplane active. "B" Battery registered various points from alternate position. Enemy shelled BECOURT. Working to report.	
— "" —	9/11/15		"D" Battery fired 17 rounds at Enemy O.P. "B" Bty fired at working Party	
— "" —	10/11/15		"C" and "E" Battries registered "Test Registration."	
— "" —	11/11/15		Battries fired in LA BOISELLE. Enemy shelled HILL 106.	

WAR DIARY
or
INTELLIGENCE SUMMARY
(Erase heading not required.)

Army Form C. 2118

Place	Date	Hour	Summary of Events and Information	Remarks and references to Appendices
BERTHE	12/11/15		Batteries fired on "Barrage Lines" for "SOS" Greenhalgh. D'Bty fired at Working Party. Enemy shelled ALBERT.	
-"-	13/11/15		Enemy shelled Medical Station at HILL 106.	
-"-	14/11/15		A Battery shelled LA BOISSELLE with 15 rounds in Retaliation. C Battery " Enemy Fire Trenches in retaliation. B Bty registered pts in LA BOISSELLE	
-"-	15/11/15		Btys fire at various points in retaliation to Trench Mortar fire.	
-"-	16/11/15		D Bty fires 6 rounds at X5 C.1.5 in retaliation.	
-"-	17/11/15		A and B Batteries registered points on LA BOISSELLE.	
-"-	18/11/15		B Battery fires 6 rounds at Working Party on LA BOISSELLE.	
-"-	19/11/15		D Bty fires 2 rounds on ALBERT.	
-"-	19/11/15		D Bty fires at Working Party and also at a Sniper's Post.	
-"-	20/11/15		Batteries fire at various Targets in LA BOISSELLE with fifteen rounds in retaliation.	
-"-	21/11/15		B Bty shelled HILL 106	
-"-	21/11/15		A, C and D Bty fired on Enemy Trenches in retaliation. B Bty fires at Working Parties. Enemy shelled ALBERT.	
-"-	22/11/15		Nothing to report.	
-"-	23/11/15		D Battery fires at Sniper's Post.	
-"-	24/11/15		A shelled enemy Trenches with 5 rounds in retaliation. C and D Bty fires at Working Parties.	
-"-	25/11/15		Enemy shelled HILL 106 with 35 rounds. Batteries shelled various Targets in retaliation. B Bty fires 11 rounds at Sniper's Post. Enemy shelled ALBERT.	

Army Form C.

WAR DIARY
or
INTELLIGENCE SUMMARY
(Erase heading not required.)

Instructions regarding War Diaries and Intelligence Summaries are contained in F.S. Regs., Part II. and the Staff Manual respectively. Title Pages will be prepared in manuscript.

Place	Date	Hour	Summary of Events and Information	Remarks and references to Appendices
BETHUNE	26/11/15		'C' Battery shelled enemy's second line trench. 'D' and 'B' Btys fired at working parties. Enemy shelled B0.15.70.19	
	27/11/15		'A' Battery fired at Snipers Post. 'B' Bty shelled LA BOISSELLE. Enemy shelled "Bedfordshire Avenue".	
-"-	28/11/15		'A' Bty fired at working party. 'B' Bty fired 5 rounds at working party in LA BOISSELLE. 'D' fired 14 rounds in retaliation.	
-"-	29/11/15		'A' Battery fired 10 rounds into snipers. 'B' Battery shelled LA BOISSELLE with 17 rounds in retaliation to Enemy T.M. fire.	
-"-	30/11/15		'C' Battery fired on working party.
Lieut-Colonel H.A. Boyce R.F.A. assumed Command of the Brigade on Nov 25/915 vice Lieut-Colonel A.F. Metcalfe D.S.O. relieved as Commandant R.A. 3rd Army	

Clyde Grant R.F.A.
for
Lieut. Colonel. R.F.A.
Comdg. 93rd Brigade Royal Field Artillery

Cp Verde, RRa.
Vol. 5

12/
7935

18th Feb

Army Form C. 2118

WAR DIARY
or
INTELLIGENCE SUMMARY
(Erase heading not required.)

83rd Bee R.F.A

Instructions regarding War Diaries and Intelligence Summaries are contained in F.S. Regs., Part II. and the Staff Manual respectively. Title Pages will be prepared in manuscript.

Place	Date	Hour	Summary of Events and Information	Remarks and references to Appendices
Bellvue	1/12/15		C. Battery fired 34 rounds on Enemy trenches.	
—	2/12/15		A. & D. Batteries fired on working parties also in retaliation. Enemy shells Hill 106.	
—	3/12/15		A. & D. Batteries again fired at Working Parties. B. Battery shelled LA BOISSELLE mk 6 rounds. Enemy fires 2 shells into ALBERT.	
—	4/12/15		from B.C. II No. 2. B. Battery fired at Enemy Wire Entanglements. A. and D. fired in retaliation.	
—	5/12/15		B. Battery fired at Machine Gun emplacement.	
—	6/12/15		C. Battery fired 16 rounds. Checking various points.	
—	7/12/15		Enemy fired 6 rounds which fell near "B." Bty position. Enemy also shelled Hill 106 and 13 rounds.	
—	8/12/15		A and C Batteries fired on enemy trenches in retaliation. Enemy fired 6 rounds which fell on Hill 106. Nothing to report.	
—	9/12/15		B and C Batteries fired at Barrage lines (for At four) B and D Batteries shelled LA BOISSELLE after we had exploded a mine.	
—	10/12/15		Enemy shells ALBERT with 5.9 rounds.	
—	11/12/15		B. Battery fires on LA BOISSELLE and POZIERES in working parties. A and D. Batteries fires at working parties.	
—	12/12/15		Enemy fires 2 shells into ALBERT.	

Army Form C. 2118

WAR DIARY
or
INTELLIGENCE SUMMARY
(Erase heading not required.)

Instructions regarding War Diaries and Intelligence Summaries are contained in F.S. Regs., Part II. and the Staff Manual respectively. Title Pages will be prepared in manuscript.

Place	Date	Hour	Summary of Events and Information	Remarks and references to Appendices
BERLUE	13/12/15		'D' Battery fires at Enemy Party. 'B' Battery fires at Enemy trenches in retaliation.	
—	14/12/15		Enemy shells HILL 106 during the day. 'B' Battery fires at working party.	
—	15/12/15		'A' Battery fires on working party. 'B' Battery shells LA BOISSELLE.	
—	16/12/15		'D' Battery shells enemy trenches in retaliation to T. Mortar fire.	
—	17/12/15		Nothing to report.	
—	—		Lt-Col. R.O. Kylie assumed command of the Brigade vice Lt-Col. Le Boyer.	
—	18/12/15		'B' Battery shells LA BOISSELLE and enemy trenches in retaliation to Enemy Trench mortar fire.	
—	19/12/15		'B' Battery shells LA BOISSELLE with 6 rounds in retaliation. 'A' & 'D' 'C' Batteries shelled enemy trenches also in retaliation. Enemy exploded two mines.	
—	19/12/15		'A' 'B' 'C' 'D' Batteries shells LA BOISSELLE and various points in retaliation. 'A' Battery fires 4 rounds at Machine Gun emplacement. Enemy exploded a mine. Enemy also fires 4 rounds near C.B.5. Redb.	
—	20/12/15		'C' Battery shells Enemy trenches in retaliation. 'C' and 'D' Battery shells LA BOISSELLE.	
—	21/12/15		Nothing to report.	
—	22/12/15		'C' Battery fires 12 rounds at sniper Post. 'B' & 'D' Batteries shelled LA BOISSELLE.	
			Enemy shelled HILL 106 during the day.	

Army Form C. 2118.

WAR DIARY
or
INTELLIGENCE SUMMARY.
(Erase heading not required.)

Instructions regarding War Diaries and Intelligence Summaries are contained in F.S. Regs., Part II and the Staff Manual respectively. Title pages will be prepared in manuscript.

Hour, Date, Place	Summary of Events and Information	Remarks and references to Appendices
Bezzue 23/12/15	'A' 'B' and 'D' Batteries shelled LA BOISSELLE in retaliation to Enemy "Minne". 'A' Bty fired at two parties. 'B' Bty fired at Snipers Post. 'C' Battery registered unknown points by aid of aeroplane. Enemy shelled ALBERT during the day.	
24/12/15	'C' Battery fired at Sniper Post and also at a Working Party. Enemy shelled "HILL 106" during the day.	
25/12/15	'B' and 'D' Batteries shelled LA BOISSELLE and POZIERES in retaliation. 'A' and 'C' Batteries fired on Enemy trenches in retaliation.	
26/12/15	Enemy shelled ALBERT during the Afternoon. 'A' Battery shelled FRICOURT WOOD with 50 rounds. 'D' Battery fired at Working Party. 'B' Battery fired at Snipers Post. Enemy shelled HILL 106 during day.	
27/12/15	'B' and 'D' Batteries shelled LA BOISSELLE in retaliation to Enemy T.M. fire. Enemy shelled HILL 106.	
29/12/15	Nothing to report.	
29/12/15	'D' Battery fired 20 minute mk LA BOISSELLE in Retaliation.	
30/12/15	'B' and 'D' Batteries shelled LA BOISSELLE. C Battery fired on Barrage Kens. Enemy shelled Wagon Kens, Killing 1 horse, wounding 1 horse, wounded 3 and also wounding 1 man.	
31/12/15	'B' Battery shelled LA BOISSELLE. Enemy shelled BELLVUE Farm and ALBERT.	

(Signed) Case Rdg
for Lieut. Colonel. R.F.A.
Comdg. 83rd Brigade Royal Field Artillery

S3rd Isaac: R.74.
tsl: 6

Army Form C. 2118.

WAR DIARY
or
INTELLIGENCE SUMMARY.
(Erase heading not required.)

153rd Brigade R.F.A.

Instructions regarding War Diaries and Intelligence Summaries are contained in F.S. Regs., Part II. and the Staff Manual respectively. Title pages will be prepared in manuscript.

Hour, Date, Place	Summary of Events and Information	Remarks and references to Appendices
BERVUE 1/1/16	Nothing to report.	
2/1/16	Lt. Col. A.F. McTaggart assumed command of the Brigade Vice Lt-Col P.D. Wylde.	
	550	
3/1/16	'B' and 'D' Batteries bombarded LA BOISSELLE after one of our mines had been exploded. 'C' Battery fired on Savage Keep in retaliation to enemy Trench Mortars.	
	'C' Battery fired at Snipers Post.	
	Enemy Shelled HILL 106.	
4/1/16	'D' Battery fired at Working Party. C. Battery fired on "Savage Keep."	
	Enemy Shelled HILL 106 with 9 rounds.	
5/1/16	'B' Battery Shelled LA BOISSELLE. 'D' Battery fired at Working Party.	
	Enemy Shelled HILL 106 with 1 round.	
6/1/16	Nothing to report.	
7/1/16	'A' Battery reached position and proceeded to BONFAY.	
	'11' Battery R.H.A. attached to Brigade and took over 'A' Battery position.	
	'D' Battery 164th Brigade attached to Brigade for course of instruction.	
	Enemy fired near Brigade Head Quarters.	
8/1/16	'B' and 'D' Battery. Enemy were entering Bonfay	
9/1/16	'B' Battery Shelled LA BOISSELLE and Working Party.	
	'D' Battery fired at M.G. emplacement and registered various points.	
	Enemy Shelled SHAMROCK Tree with 10 rounds.	
10/1/16	Nothing to report.	
11/1/16	'D' Battery fired at Working Party. C. By. fired 4 rounds. "Wire Cutting"	

WAR DIARY / INTELLIGENCE SUMMARY

Army Form C. 2118.

83rd Brigade R.F.A.

Hour, Date, Place	Summary of Events and Information	Remarks and references to Appendices
B-22 Rue Farm 12/1/16	"D" Battery fired at "Snipers Post". Enemy shelled Shamrock tree.	
13/1/16	"C" Battery fired 25 rounds cutting Enemy wire entanglements. "B" and "D" Batteries shelled Enemy Communication trenches (Inspekers Relay). Enemy shelled ALBERT and FERME BELLVUE with 15 rounds.	
14/1/16	Nothing to report.	
15/1/16	"B" Battery fired 9 rounds into LA BOISSELLE.	
16/1/16	"B" Battery shelled LA BOISSELLE.	
	"C" and "D" Batteries shelled enemy trenches.	
17/1/16	"D" Battery fired 7 rounds at Communication trenches near LA BOISSELLE. Enemy aeroplanes active during the morning.	
18/1/16	"C" Battery shelled enemy's front trenches fired 25 rounds. Enemy shelled Shamrock tree and vicinity of Brigade Head Quarters.	
19/1/16	"B" and "D" shelled LA BOISSELLE. D/164 moved to TREUX	
20/1/16	Nothing to report	
21/1/16	B.C-D shelled LA BOISSELLE and enemy trenches Enemy shelled trenches	
22/1/16	B-D shelled emplacements at X 14 A 32, 99 and working parties Enemy shelled BECOURT- ALBERT Road & Shamrock tree Aid	

Army Form C. 2118.

WAR DIARY
INTELLIGENCE SUMMARY.
(Erase heading not required.)

83rd Bde Bgde R.F.A.

Hour, Date, Place	Summary of Events and Information	Remarks and references to Appendices
BELLEVUE FARM 23.1.16	Lt. Col. Metcalfe took command of 18Div R.A. during absence Army shelled Shamrock Tree at intervals from 10am to 4pm	B.G. Van Straubenzee assumed command and
24.1.16	and ALBERT - BECOURT road during the morning. Major R.B. Boyd of 83rd Bde RFA	
	Batteries shelled LA BOISSELLE, Y Sap and registered points	
	Enemy trench mortars very active	
25.1.16	Batteries fired at working parties, snipers posts and in retaliation	
	to trench mortars.	
	Enemy aeroplane flew over our lines dropping bombs on	
26.1.16	DERNANCOURT. Our enemy observation balloons on	
	13. Battery shelled LA BOISSELLE with 37 rounds.	
	Enemy shelled Shamrock Tree at intervals during the day. They also	
	shelled a French Aeroplane which had been forced to descend near	
	Brigade Head Quarters.	
27.1.16	D. and C. Batteries bombarded enemy wire entanglements	
	Enemy shelled Shamrock Tree and Secln XII.	
	They also fired 14 rounds into ALBERT.	
28.1.16	C. Battery fired 15 rounds on "Barrage lines"	
	Enemy fired 5 rounds on Shamrock Tree.	
29.1.16	C. Battery fired 25 rounds at Enemy front trenches	
	from 2.20 to 4pm Enemy shelled our trenches in E"with 9.0 rounds.	
30.1.16	Enemy shelled ALBERT with 35 rounds during the morning.	
	13. Battery shelled LA BOISSELLE with 11 rounds.	

Army Form C. 2118.

WAR DIARY
or
INTELLIGENCE SUMMARY.
(Erase heading not required.)

Hour, Date, Place	Summary of Events and Information	Remarks and references to Appendices
Bellevue FARM 31.1.16	'B' 'C' and 'D' Batteries shelled Enemy Trenches heavily between 5pm and 6.20pm in reply to Heavy Bombardment by the enemy on Sector E II. 'A' Battery returned from Bonnay and took over position from 4 Battery R.H.A.	93rd Brigade R.F.A. E. Clyde Neuve R.F.A Adjt 83rd Bde R.F.A

1916(?)

83rd Bde RFA   Army Form C. 2118.

WAR DIARY
INTELLIGENCE SUMMARY
(Erase heading not required.)

Hour, Date, Place	Summary of Events and Information	Remarks and references to Appendices
Ber2 Vue Ferme 1/2/15	D. Battery fired 100 rounds at Enemy's Wire entanglements. Enemy Shelled Sectn E.II at intervals during the day.	
2/2/15	A. Bty. Registered various points by aid of Aeroplane. B. Bty. Shelled LA BOISSELLE with 25 rounds. Enemy Shelled Kinchs in E.III Sectr. and also fired 5 rounds at Shamrock Tree.	
3/2/15	D. Battery fired 20 rounds at various points. A. Battery Registered point X.11.a.5.99 by aid of Aeroplane.	
4/2/15	Enemy Shelled Shamrock Tree and Trenches in E.II Sut Sectr. All Batteries Bombarded Enemy Trenches (Combined Bombardment) Enemy Shelled Trenches in E.III Sub Sectr with 40 rounds	
5/2/15	All Batteries again bombarded Enemy Trenches (600 rounds in all, being fired) Enemy Biplane flew over position at 11am. Enemy Shelled Sub Sectr E.III	
6/2/15	All Batteries again bombarded Enemy Trenches, with 570 rounds. Enemy Shelled E2 and E3 Sub Sectrs heavily during the day. Enemy fired 4 rounds at Shamrock Tree	
7/2/15	D. Battery fired 15 rounds at Enemy working Parties. Enemy Shelled Trenches in E.II and E.III during the day.	
8/2/15	Bombarded Party of Germans seen. D. Battery fired at ALBERT with 20 rounds and also Enemy Shelled ALBERT with 20 rounds and also Enemy Shelled Trenches in E.2 and E.3 heavily during the day.	
9/2/15		

WAR DIARY
or
INTELLIGENCE SUMMARY.
(Erase heading not required.)

Army Form C. 2118.

Instructions regarding War Diaries and Intelligence Summaries are contained in F.S. Regs., Part II. and the Staff Manual respectively. Title pages will be prepared in manuscript.

Hour, Date, Place	Summary of Events and Information	Remarks and references to Appendices
Bellevue Farm. 10-2-16	'A' and 'D' Batteries Registered. 'B' Battery shelled Shamrock Tree and Sectn E III.	'B' Battery shelled A.1.9 B.0.1.5.5 & 7.7.2 with 15 rounds.
" 11-2-16.	'B' Battery fired 10 rounds into A.1.9 B.0.1.5.5 & 7.7.2. 'C' Battery checked Barrage lines. Enemy shelled Sectn E III throughout the day.	
" 12-2-16.	'B' Battery fired 5 rounds into A.1.9 B.0.1.5.5 & 7.7.2. 'A' C' and D' Batteries fired at enemy trenches Sectn E III, 12 rounds falling near D Battery.	
" 13-2-16	Enemy again shelled Sectn E III. Nothing to Report.	
" 14-2-16	'B' and 'D' Batteries fired on Enemy trenches in conjunction with Mine.	
" 15-2-16	'C' Battery Registered Barrage Lines in Sectn E III. Enemy shelled trenches in Sectn E III. 'C' Battery again Registered new Barrages. 'B' Battery fired at working Party. 'D' Battery fired on Enemy Trenches.	
" 16-2-16	Enemy shelled trenches in Sectn E III. 'D' Battery fired 250 rounds on Enemy trenches in co-operation with scheme of 32nd Divisional Artillery.	
" 17-2-16	'D' and 'C' Battery wagon lines moved to Riunu. 'A' Battery checked Barrage Lines. Enemy shelled various points in Sectn E III.	
" 18-2-16	Nothing to Report.	
" 19-2-16	'C' and 'D' Batteries fired at working Parties. Enemy shelled Sectn E III heavily throughout the day. Aeroplane flew over ALBERT at 11-5-0 pm and dropped 2 white lights	

(73989) W4141—463. 400,000. 9/14. H.&J.Ltd. Forms/C. 2118/10.

WAR DIARY

INTELLIGENCE SUMMARY

(Erase heading not required.)

Army Form C. 2118

Instructions regarding War Diaries and Intelligence Summaries are contained in F.S. Regs, Part II. and the Staff Manual respectively. Title Pages will be prepared in manuscript.

Place	Date	Hour	Summary of Events and Information	Remarks and references to Appendices
Bellevue Farme	20/2/16		'B' Battery registered New Barrage Lines. Enemy shelled Shamrock Tree and Bécourt.	
—	21/2/16		'A' Battery registered ? for mutual support with 7th Division. 'D' Battery registered new Barrages and shelled enemy dug-outs. 'B' Battery registered trench North of LA BOISSELLE. Enemy shelled Bois No.19.	
—	22/2/16		'A' Battery fired 327 rounds to assist 7th Division in repelling an Enemy attack. They also fired 12 rounds which fell near Bus Head trenches attempted on our trenches and mine shafts.	
—	23/2/16		'B' Battery and 'D' Battery fired at Machine Gun emplacements. Enemy shelling trenches and Battery positions throughout the day.	
—	24/2/16		'C' Battery fired at Enemy working Party. 'C' Battery fired 27 rounds at a M.G. Emplacement and destroyed it. 'D' Battery fired at working Party in LA BOISSELLE.	
—	25/2/16		Enemy Aeroplane flew over position at 3pm and dropped bomb on TARA HILL. Nothing to report.	
—	26/2/16		'D' Battery fired 19 rounds at Enemy posts trenches clearing trenches of Snow. Enemy fired 36 rounds at Lochnagar Dump.	
—	27/2/16		Nothing to report	

Army Form C. 2118

WAR DIARY
INTELLIGENCE SUMMARY
(Erase heading not required.)

Place	Date	Hour	Summary of Events and Information	Remarks and references to Appendices
Bellevue Ferme	28/2/16		D Battery fires at Working Party. Enemy Artillery active throughout the day.	
—	29/2/16		'B', 'C' and 'D' Batteries fires at working Parties. 'C' Battery fires to check Barrage Lines. Enemy shells Biscuit Wood, Shamrock Tree and Trenches. 'A' Battery fires 200 rounds. Mutine Support with 71st Division.	

for Lieut. Colonel R.F.A.
Comdg. 53rd Br. 2) Roy. J.H.R Artillery

U 18
83R FA
Vol 8

Army Form C. 2118

WAR DIARY

~~INTELLIGENCE SUMMARY~~

(Erase heading not required.)

[Stamp: 63RD BRIGADE ROYAL FIELD ARTILLERY]

Place	Date	Hour	Summary of Events and Information	Remarks and references to Appendices
Bell Vue Farm	1/3/16		Nothing to report.	
	2/3/16		Nothing to report.	
	3/3/16		The whole Brigade went into 'Reserve' at DAOURS (La Somme) via BUIRE. The Brigade halted at BUIRE for the night Mar 3/4, 1916, and proceeded to DAOURS at 9am Mar 4th, 1916. The 32nd Divisional Artillery took over the position of the Brigade at 10am Mar 3/1916.	
	4/3/16		The Brigade reached DAOURs during the afternoon.	
	5/3/16		Nothing to report	
	6/3/16		— // —	
	7/3/16		'B' and 'D' Batteries proceeded to SUZANNE where they went into action with the 150th Brigade R.F.A. 30th Division.	
	8/3/16 to 21/3/16		Nothing to report.	
Bray	22/3/16		'A' and 'C' Batteries left DAOURS and proceeded to Bray. The Brigade took over the frontage held by 150th Bde R.F.A. 'B' and 'D' Bdes rejoined Brigade. B/150, B/151, and D/15" attached to Brigade to form the centre group of 17th Div. Art.	

WAR DIARY

INTELLIGENCE SUMMARY

Army Form C. 2118

(Erase heading not required.)

Place	Date	Hour	Summary of Events and Information	Remarks and references to Appendices
Bray	23/3/16		"D" Battery registered Enemy's front line Trench	
	24/3/16		A and C Batteries registered known points in Enemy's line.	
	25/3/16		The Bde Amm. Col. left Daours and proceeded to the Bois Des Tailles	
	26/3/16		Enemy shelled Maricourt Wood. Several shells fell near A/83	
	27/3/16		Enemy shelled Maricourt Wood and "Castle Ave"	
	28/3/16		"A" Bty fired on Enemy working parties and also registered various pts. A and C Btys shelled Enemy trenches in retaliation for the shelling of Maricourt and our trenches.	
	29/3/16		A Bty fired at Enemy working party. A and C Btys registered various points. Enemy Artillery very active throughout the Day. Two Enemy aeroplanes flew over position. C Bty registered junctions of Enemy trenches.	
	30/3/16		Enemy shelled Eponne Rd, Suzanne - Carnoy Rd and Maricourt Wood. The valleys near Suzanne were heavily shelled by the enemy throughout the day. D Bty fired on snipers post and M.G. emplacement Enemy shelled Billon Wood, upper A Wood and Suzanne and Maricourt Rd.	
	31/3/16			

C Goodlet R.F.A.
1st Lieut - ?
Commdg 83rd Brigade R.F.A.

Army Form C. 2118

WAR DIARY or INTELLIGENCE SUMMARY

(Erase heading not required.)

XVIII
53rd Brigade R.F.A. Vol 9

Place	Date	Hour	Summary of Events and Information	Remarks and references to Appendices
BRAY	1/4/16		'B' Battery fired at Enemy Transport. 'C' Bty fired on Enemy Communication Trenches. Enemy shelled Carnoy, MARICOURT, SUZANNE and PERONNE Rd.	
-"-	2/4/16		'A' and 'C' Btys registered "Zones". 'D' Bty fired at M.G. emplacements. Enemy shelled MARICOURT. Bty also fired a few rounds which fell near A/83 position.	
-"-	3/4/16		'B' and 'D' Batteries registered points in Enemy Trenches. 'C' Bty fired Harrass on Working Party. Enemy shelled Billon Wood and MARICOURT throughout the day. Machine Gun took 'C' Battery registered enemy front line. 'B' Battery fired Harrass at M.G. emplacement.	
-"-	4/4/16		Enemy shelled TALUS BOISÉ, MARICOURT Wood and PERONNE Rd.	
-"-	5/4/16		'D' Bty fired on Enemy front line trenches in PETAIRBIN. Enemy shelled BILLON Wood with 40 rounds.	
-"-	6/4/16		'A' 'B' and 'D' Batteries registered various points in enemy trenches. Enemy shelled COPSE M, MARICOURT and Valleys round SUZANNE.	
-"-	7/4/16		'A' Bty registered Enemys front line trench. 'C' Battery fired at Snipers Post. Enemy shelled 'U' Works and Suzanne – MARICOURT Valley. 'D' Bty fired at Emplacement for Trench Mortar machine. (Emplacement destroyed.)	
-"-	8/4/16		'A' Bty fired 10 rounds at Enemy Working Party. 'D' Bty fired on Enemy Trenches in Petairbin. 'D' Bty fired from Carlanni Post Enemy shelled PERONNE Rd with 36 rounds.	
-"-	9/4/16		'A' 'B' and 'C' Batteries firing on enemy Trenches and valleys round MARICOURT and SUZANNE. The Enemy Shelled the roads and valleys round MARICOURT throughout the day.	

Army Form C. 2118

WAR DIARY
or
INTELLIGENCE SUMMARY
(Erase heading not required.)

53rd Brigade R.F.A.

Instructions regarding War Diaries and Intelligence Summaries are contained in F.S. Regs., Part II. and the Staff Manual respectively. Title Pages will be prepared in manuscript.

Place	Date	Hour	Summary of Events and Information	Remarks and references to Appendices
Bray	10/4/16		'C' Battery fired at Enemy Trenches in retaliation.	
"	11/4/16		Enemy again shelled roads and valleys around MARICOURT and SUZANNE. Enemy shelled MARICOURT WOOD and PERONNE Rd. 1 Gunner of C/83 killed.	
"	12/4/16		'A', 'C' and 'D' Batteries fired on Enemy Trenches in retaliation.	
"	13/4/16		Enemy bombarded valleys around SUZANNE heavily throughout the day. 'C' Bty fired 50 rounds on Enemy support trench in retaliation. Enemy shelled MARICOURT, PERONNE Rd and MARICOURT WOOD.	
"	14/4/16		'B' Bty fired 16 rounds Testing Barrage fire. C Bty fired at Enemy working party. Enemy shelled Copse 17 with 50 rounds and ground round Bty position with 100 rounds.	
"	15/4/16		'A' and 'C' Btys registered points in Enemy trenches. 'B' Bty fired at working party. Enemy very quiet.	
"	16/4/16		'A' Bty fired at and destroyed Snipers Post. 'B' Bty fired at Enemy working Party. C Battery registered Trench Junction. Enemy shelled MARICOURT, MANINCAMP, Copse L and valleys round SUZANNE. Enemy Air Craft very active.	

WAR DIARY
INTELLIGENCE SUMMARY
(Erase heading not required.)

Army Form C. 2118

53rd Brigade R.F.A.

Place	Date	Hour	Summary of Events and Information	Remarks and references to Appendices
Bray	17/4/16		All Btys fired on Enemy front and support trenches in retaliation for heavy bombardment of our trenches by the Enemy.	
"	18/4/16		Enemy shelled MARICOURT Wood, BULON Wood, Ox Farm Copse, and road to K2. A and C Btys fired on Barrage lines (Totoy).	
"	19/4/16		Enemy shelled MARICOURT, MARICOURT Wood, Bulon Wood and M. Works. B, C and D Batteries fired on retaliation on the enemy bombardment of our trenches by the Enemy. Enemy also shelled MARICOURT, MARICOURT Wood, Peronne Rd and SUZANNE Valley.	
"	20/4/16		F Bty fires 12 rounds Testing Barrage lines. D Bty fires on Enemy trenches (Ratahetm). Enemy Artillery active throughout the day. MARICOURT and Valleys from Suzanne being heavily shelled.	
"	21/4/16		B, C and D Batteries fires on Enemy trenches (Ratahetm). Enemy shelled MARICOURT Wood, Peronne Rd and Ground round Bty positions. A 13 + C Battery shelled Enemy Trenches in Ratahetm. D Bty shelled trenches at night. Enemy shelled MARICOURT Wood, Peronne Rd and valleys round Suzanne heavily throughout the day.	

Army Form C. 2118

WAR DIARY
INTELLIGENCE SUMMARY
(Erase heading not required.)

Instructions regarding War Diaries and Intelligence Summaries are contained in F.S. Regs., Part II. and the Staff Manual respectively. Title Pages will be prepared in manuscript.

83rd Brigade R.F.A.

Place	Date	Hour	Summary of Events and Information	Remarks and references to Appendices
Bray	23/4/16		A and C Btys registered.	
-"-	24/4/16		Enemy shelled Maricourt Wood, valleys about Suzanne and Copse "U". Enemy shells valleys about Maricourt and Suzanne heavily throughout the day.	
-"-	25/4/16		A and C Batteries fired on Enemy Trenches in retaliation. C and B Batteries registered points in Enemy Lines.	
-"-	26/4/16		Enemy shelled Talus Boisé, Lapré Wood, Bulln Wood and valleys about Suzanne. B Battery fired at and destroyed M.G. Emplacement. A & D Batteries bombarded Enemy Trenches. Aviating Infantry in "Raid" Enemy shelled Cerisy Rd, Talus Boisé, Bulln Wood, Maricourt Wood and our trenches in reply to our bombardment.	
-"-	27/4/16		A and C Batteries registered points in Enemy Trenches. Enemy shelled ground about Suzanne and Maricourt.	
-"-	28/4/16		A and D Batteries fired at Working Parties. Enemy Artillery active throughout the day.	
-"-	29/4/16		A and C Batteries registered various points. D Battery fired at Working Party. Enemy shelled Lapré Wood, Bulln Wood, and Talus Boisé.	

Army Form C. 2118

53rd Brigade RFA

WAR DIARY
or
INTELLIGENCE SUMMARY

(Erase heading not required.)

53rd Brigade RFA

Instructions regarding War Diaries and Intelligence Summaries are contained in F.S. Regs., Part II. and the Staff Manual respectively. Title Pages will be prepared in manuscript.

Place	Date	Hour	Summary of Events and Information	Remarks and references to Appendices
Bray	30/4/16		A.B.C. and D. Batteries fired on Enemy trenches in retaliation to heavy bombardment of our own trenches by the Enemy. Enemy shelled Mariscourt, Mariscourt Wood, Peronne Rd and "Sector A2".	

C. Lyon C RFA
Adj: for Lt Col
Comdg 53rd Brigade R.F.A.

WAR DIARY
or
INTELLIGENCE SUMMARY

(Erase heading not required.)

Army Form C. 2118

XVIII VOL 10
83rd Brigade R.F.A.

Place	Date	Hour	Summary of Events and Information	Remarks and references to Appendices
Bray	1/5/16		"A" Battery shelled Bois des Haut in Peronne. "A" Battery fired on Enemy working party.	
"	2/5/16		Enemy shelled Talus Boise, Large Wood, W.Works and Copse "N". "A" Battery shelled Trucks Wood in Peronne.	
"			Enemy shelled German troop Battery positions and Maricourt – Suzanne Valley.	
"	3/5/16		"D" Battery fired on enemy trenches, checking Registration.	
"			Enemy shelled Maricourt Wood, Peronne Rd and our Support Trenches.	
"	4/5/16		"C" Battery destroyed a Sniper's Post.	
"			"B" "C" and "D" Batteries bombarded "Barrage Lines" in reply to Enemy Bombardment of our Trenches by the Enemy.	
"			Enemy bombarded Trenches south of Peronne Rd, Maricourt Wood, Billon Wood and Valleys from Suzanne very heavily.	
"	5/5/16		"C" Battery registered various points. "A" Battery fired on Enemy Trenches.	
"			Enemy again bombarded Maricourt Wood and Valleys heavily.	
"	6/5/16		The Brigade Ammunition Column were relieved by the 150th B.A.C., and left the Bois des Tailles on route for Arboeures arriving at the later place the same day.	

Army Form C. 2118

83rd Brigade R.F.A.

WAR DIARY or INTELLIGENCE SUMMARY

Place	Date	Hour	Summary of Events and Information	Remarks and references to Appendices
Bray	6/7/16	9pm	Batteries of the Brigade were relieved by Batteries of the 152nd Brigade R.F.A. 'B','C' and 'D' Batteries proceeded to wagon lines in Bois des TAILLES, leaving here for the night. A Battery handed position over to C/148 and took up new position under command of OC Left Group 18th Divl. Art. Bee HQ the until 'B','C' and 'D' Batteries left Bois des Taillis en route for the Reserve Area, ARGOEUVES, via DAOURS, reaching ARGOEUVES same afternoon. The Front held by Centre Group 15th Divl Art was handed over to Centre Group 30th Divl Art at 5 a.m. 7/7/1916.	
ARGOEUVES	7/5/16	5am		
	24/5/16		On re-organization of Div. BAC became No 1 Sec Echelon A. 18 Div. D/83 became B/85 and D/85 became D/83. Brigade now consists of 3 18 pr and 1 4.5" How Batteries. A/83 (old D/85) has been in action while Bde is at rest, attached to Left group 30th Div R.A.	
	26/5/16		B/83 marched at 5 a.m. to take up position near BILLON WOOD and since be attached to 30 Div R.A. Special order of the day by G.O.C. in chief B.E.F received congratulating the regiment on attaining two years service formation	

Army Form C. 2118

WAR DIARY
or
INTELLIGENCE SUMMARY
(Erase heading not required.)

83rd Brigade RFA

Instructions regarding War Diaries and Intelligence Summaries are contained in F.S. Regs., Part II. and the Staff Manual respectively. Title Pages will be prepared in manuscript.

Place	Date	Hour	Summary of Events and Information	Remarks and references to Appendices
MARICOURT VALLEY	28th & 29th 5/76		During night 28-29th a new trench was dug from A9D 20.20 to A16A 20.76. The trench was cleaned on the morning of 29th and registered by A/83. The enemy retaliated heavily. In retaliation C/83 fired 150 rounds.	
	30		Nothing to report	
	31		Brigade HQ and C/83 at rest in ARGOUVES A, B and D Btys in action in vicinity of BILLON WOOD attached A to left group 18 Div, B and D to centre group 30 Div	

Signed E. RFA
for Lt Col RFA
Comdg 83rd Bde RFA

D/23 RFA
(18) VOL 1
Army Form C. 2118

WAR DIARY or INTELLIGENCE SUMMARY

(Erase heading not required.)

Instructions regarding War Diaries and Intelligence Summaries are contained in F.S. Regs., Part II. and the Staff Manual respectively. Title Pages will be prepared in manuscript.

Place	Date	Hour	Summary of Events and Information	Remarks and references to Appendices
SUZANNE	1/5/16		Work started on No. 2 Gun-pit. Rw.9	
	2.5.16		140 Rounds 10.5 cm 13 cm fell near at B.D. Hersey position Rw.9	
	3.5.16		8 Rounds to find and registration of new targets No. 4 gun had a permanent Rw.9	MARICOURT 62° N.W. 1:10,000
	4.5.16		Rw.9	ant
	5.5.16		Rw.9	
	6.5.16		Rw.9	
	7.5.16 7 ohm		Enemy shelled tracks in front of Bolting Rw.9	
	8.5.16		Fired 12 Rds on transport tracks at S. 28 A.i.B in retaliation Rw.9	LONGUEVAL 57° S.W. 2
	9.5.16		Fired 57 Rds in retaliation for enemy shelling our front line. Rw.9	
	10.5.16		Fired 58 Rds. in retaliation for enemy shelling A16.2.79 and fired 53 Rds on MONTAUBAN Rw.9	1:10,000
	11.5.16		Fired 15 Rds for the purpose of testing the range of N.C.T charge Rw.9	
	12.5.16		Fired 6 Rds in retaliation. Rw.9	
	13.5.16 1 A.M		Some Lachrymatory shells fell near Battery. We fired 54 rds in retaliation? Rw.9	
	14.5.16		Rw.9	
	15.5.16		Rw.9	
	16.5.16		Rw.9	
	17.5.16		Fired 75 Rds observation done by aeroplane. Rw.9	
	18.5.16		Good day for observation. Fired 16 Rds at MALTZ HORN FARM A6 a 9530 Rw.9	
	19.5.16		Fired 21 Rds. observed by aeroplane Rw.9	
	20.5.16		Fired 25 rds for enemy shelling front line trenches Rw.9	
	21.5.16		Work on No. 2 gun-pit continued. Rw.9	
	22.5.16		Rw.9	
	23.5.16		Rw.9	

Army Form C. 2118

WAR DIARY
or
INTELLIGENCE SUMMARY
(Erase heading not required.)

Instructions regarding War Diaries and Intelligence Summaries are contained in F. S. Regs., Part II. and the Staff Manual respectively. Title Pages will be prepared in manuscript.

Place	Date	Hour	Summary of Events and Information	Remarks and references to Appendices
	24.5.16		200 Rds. 10.5 cm. and 15 cm. fell near Battery. Battery changed its name to "D/83" from 12 mm today. Regt.	
	25.5.16		30 Rds. 10.5 cm. fell near Battery Regt.	
	26.5.16		Rwt.	
	27.5.16		Rwt.	
	28.5.16		Rwt.	
	29.5.16		Fired 130 rds. in retaliation for enemy shelling our front line Rwt.	
	30.5.16		Fired 90 rds. in retaliation for enemy shelling our front line Rwt.	
	31.5.16		Rwt.	

J.P. Sheen Capt. R.H.A.
Comdg. "D"/83rd Bde. R.H.A.

WAR DIARY or INTELLIGENCE SUMMARY

83rd Bde R.F.A.

Army Form C. 2118

(Erase heading not required.)

Place	Date	Hour	Summary of Events and Information	Remarks and references to Appendices
ARGOEUVES	1/6/16		A, B and D Batteries in action in neighbourhood of MARICOURT and CARNOY attached to Cape French 18 Div and Curtis French 30 Div. C Bty and Bde H.Q. at ARGOEUVES	
	2/6/16 to 9/6/16		Nothing to report. Bt Col J.O. Sacgnam assumed Command vice Brig Gen S.F. METCALFE	
	10/6/16		Bde H.Q. and C/83 received orders to march to take up position billeted at CORBIE	
	11/6/16		Bde H.Q. and C/83 marched to BOIS des TAILLES and remained there until dark, then marched to positions. We are now Left Corps Centre Group, 18 Div R.A. with seven Batteries A, B, C, D/83, B/85 and two batteries of 9th Div. Positions for Batteries are being prepared.	
	12/6/16		Zones on whole front allotted and orders re wire cutting issued to Battery Commanders.	
	13/6/16 to 19/6/16		Batteries engaged registering German wire, Communication trenches and approaches. Positions are A/83 A 2 c 48 21 C/83 A 2 c 30.30 D/83 A 26 D 8.9 B/85 A 19 D 4.6 B/83 F 23 c 85 40 D/50 A 25 B 2.4 B/50 F 23 D 2.4 C/51 A 15 D 7.9 Reference MARICOURT and MEAULTE Sheet	

Army Form C. 2118

WAR DIARY 83rd Bde R.F.A.

INTELLIGENCE SUMMARY

(Erase heading not required.)

Instructions regarding War Diaries and Intelligence Summaries are contained in F. S. Regs, Part II. and the Staff Manual respectively. Title Pages will be prepared in manuscript.

Place	Date	Hour	Summary of Events and Information	Remarks and references to Appendices
BILLON WOOD	19/6/16		Wire to be cut by Batteries in front of German trenches from A8.A.80.35 to A7.B.55.60 and extends north by E or for on MONTAUBAN ALLEY (Ref MARICOURT Sheet). This is divided into 5 Zones numbered 1.2.3.4.5 from E to W. The Batteries to engage the Zones (called wire cutting batteries) are A/83 (1) C/83 (2) B/83 (3) B/50 (4) B/83 (5), and 3 days are allotted to the task. These Batteries are also responsible for the defence of the Zones by night and will prevent repair of wire cut. D/83 will engage all machine gun and I.M positions in the Zones and communication trenches. C/51 will not fire until the Infantry have advanced. They will then form a barrage S. of CATERPILLAR WOOD. A/83 and B/85 are selected to move forward in case of an advance and position has been selected for them at A14.A.6-1. (A/83) and A.14.A.4-7. B/85. Two Liaison Officers have been detailed to accompany the Battalion in the Advance.	
20/6/16 21/6/16 22/6/16 23/6/16 24/6/16		Batteries registered	
	25/6/16		"U" Day A,B,C/63 B/65 and B/50 engaged enemy wire on outpost trenches and good results and B/83 and B/50 (18pdrs) and D/83 4.5" How fired at irregular intervals during the night on Communication trenches and strong points. Practically no reply from enemy. Heavy Artillery firing all day and night. Orders received that SUFFOLKS would carry out a raid on enemy trenches at midnight. Wire to be cut by X.15 I.M Bty assisted by 18pdrs of 16 Armoury. B/83 and B/50 to put barrage on selected portion of enemy trenches. During raid and wire cutting enemy retaliated very slightly.	

Vol 11
83rd Bde R.F.A.
June
XVII

WAR DIARY
INTELLIGENCE SUMMARY

Place	Date	Hour	Summary of Events and Information	Remarks and references to Appendices
BILLON WOOD	26/6/16		Bombardment and wire cutting continues. Suffolks carried out a raid on enemy trenches last night on a front of front line here by enemy. No prisoners taken.	
-"-	27/6/16		X day. Bombardment and wire cutting continues. Enemy are replying on our trenches and road crossings; but not vigorously.	
-"-	28/6/16		Y day. Bombardment continues, wire almost entirely cut on enemy 1st support, and 2nd line trenches. MAMETZ and MONTAUBAN villages have been heavily bombarded, effect very visible. Orders received that attack postponed 48 hours. Programme as per X and Y day to be continued on 29th and 30th (Y.1. and Y.2. days). Infantry to carry out night raids and Heavy Artillery to continue bombardment.	
-"-	29/6/16		Y.1. day. Bombardment continues. Enemy retaliation more pronounced. Equipment wearing very well, expect suffer shrings which are giving some trouble.	
-"-	30/6/16		Y.2. day. Bombardment continues. Practically no enemy wire has disappeared and his trenches have been partially demolished. Infantry on our front 53rd Inf Bde, right 55th Inf Bde, left 54th Inf Bde, right of Right of 18 Div in 30 Div, left in 7th Div. French troops from right of 30th Div.	

P. Gate C.R.F.A.
Adjt for Lieut Col R.F.A.
Comdg 83rd Bde R.F.A.

18/ vol 12

83rd Bde.
R.F.A.

July 1916

Army Form C. 2118

WAR DIARY
INTELLIGENCE SUMMARY
83rd Brigade R.F.A.

(Erase heading not required.)

Instructions regarding War Diaries and Intelligence Summaries are contained in F. S. Regs., Part II. and the Staff Manual respectively. Title Pages will be prepared in manuscript.

Place	Date	Hour	Summary of Events and Information	Remarks and references to Appendices
BILLON WOOD	1.7.16		"Z" day. Barometer 29.74 Thermometer 59. Attack on German trenches ordered for 7.30 a.m. 83rd Bde R.F.A. is supporting 53rd Inf Bde 8th NORFOLK Regt on right, 6th BERKS on left with 8th SUFFOLKS and 10th ESSEX in reserve. The front allotted to 53rd Inf Bde was divided into five zones and Covered by Batteries of this group by "A/83", "C/83" "D/83" "B/80 and "D/82" 18-pounder batteries with D/83 4.5" How itzer battery covering the whole front.	Operation Order No 1 with appendices ABC & D (1)
		6.25 am	German front line was bombarded, last five minutes intense	
		7.26		
		7.30	Infantry emerged from our trenches and attacked German front line, our barrage at this time having been lifted to German support trenches	Map (2) showing our own and German trenches and Artillery lifts.
		7.33	Our Infantry entered enemy front trench. Enemy artillery practically silent	
		7.34	Barrage lifted on to BUND SUPPORT and BACK TRENCH	
		7.39	Barrage lifted on to POMMIERS TRENCH and MINE ALLEY. Infantry progressing	
		7.49	Barrage lifted on to LOOP TRENCH and BLIND ALLEY. Reported that Infantry are hung up at THE LOOP	
		8.28	Barrage lifted on the TWINS and MONTAUBAN ALLEY. Reported that Infantry on side held up at the LOOP	
		9.5	POMMIERS TRENCH taken	
		9.52	THE LOOP taken	
		10.3	POMMIERS REDOUBT taken, MONTAUBAN ALLEY still held out	
		11.0	German Battery reported at S.26.6.0.5. "C/83" and "D/83 ordered to engage it	
		2.50	MONTAUBAN ALLEY in holding out "A/83 and "C/83 ordered to barrage than zones on MONTAUBAN ALLEY	

Army Form C. 2118

WAR DIARY
or
INTELLIGENCE SUMMARY

83rd Brigade R.F.A.

(Erase heading not required.)

Place	Date	Hour	Summary of Events and Information	Remarks and references to Appendices
BILLON WOOD	1/7/16	5.20 a.m	MONTAUBAN ALLEY taken and our infantry advance to their final objective.	
		6.30 a.m	"A"/83 moved forward to new position at A.14.a.6.1. Enemy removing guns and retiring near the gallop. Two salvoes fired by each battery at road S.19.d – S.20.c.	
		8 a.m	D/83 moved forward to new position at A.14.a.4.7. During night our infantry consolidated final objective and guns were laid on S. edge of CATERPILLAR WOOD. No serious bombardment or counter attacks by enemy during day or night.	
	2/7/16		Enemy shelled our new front line heavily during the day, work on consolidation of new line proceeding. Batteries fired at fleeting targets such as groups of enemy infantry retiring from MAMETZ WOOD. D/83 scattered teams and detachment of a field battery and prevented the guns being removed.	
	3/7/16		Batteries again had fleeting targets. German Infantry retiring before the advance of Division on our left. New forward observation stations selected for all Batteries and lines laid out and visual station (where possible) established. Forward position in CARNOY selected for D/83. Orders received that 10th ESSEX would occupy CATERPILLAR WOOD at 4-30 a.m. Artillery support arranged for.	
	4/7/16	4.30 a.m	CATERPILLAR WOOD occupied, no opposition. One 77 m.m gun and one machine gun taken. Sentry parties entered MARLBORO WOOD and later it was occupied by Suffolks. There are 5 guns of R.O.G. in CATERPILLAR WOOD, everything points to a hurried retreat on the part of the enemy. An attempt was made at 11-30 h m to withdraw the guns but the ground was found too slack.	

Army Form C. 2118

WAR DIARY
or
INTELLIGENCE SUMMARY 83rd Bde R.F.A.

(Erase heading not required.)

Place	Date	Hour	Summary of Events and Information	Remarks and references to Appendices
BILLON WOOD	4.7.16	11.30 p.m.	D/83 occupied new position in CARNOY	
	5.7.16		Position for cutting wire on German 2nd line reconnoitred	
		4.30 p.m.	C/83 occupied new position E of CARNOY	
	6.7.16		Batteries fired at fleeting targets during the day and at German 2nd line during the night to prevent work going on. A/83 secured several hits on retreating Germans. Orders received that Artillery of 3rd Div would fire wire on German 2nd line. They are expected to take up positions on night of 7/8th. 18 Div Batteries remain to defence. On same night 18 Div Infantry will be relieved by 3rd Div. B/50 and D/50 rejoined 9th Div. Team went out and brought in German guns. Orders received that 38th Div was to relieve 7th Div on our left. Preliminary bombardment of MAMETZ WOOD ordered.	(3)
	7.7.16	7.40 am to 7.30 am	Preliminary bombardment of MAMETZ WOOD 'A', C/83, D/83 toward edge of wood from N.E. corner to S.E. corner and D/83 4.5" How fires on crossroads at x.24 a 85.98	18 Div R.A. Operation Orders No. 3 and No. 2.
		7.50 am to 8.30 am	To co-operate in attack on MAMETZ WOOD by XV Corps, batteries fired on SABOT and FLATIRON Copses and on hedge between FLATIRON and S.14.D 42.14	
		10.50 to 11.15	Bombardment renewed.	
		11.30	All fire turned on to SABOT and FLATIRON Copses	

Army Form C. 2118

WAR DIARY
or
INTELLIGENCE SUMMARY   83rd Bde R.F.A.

(Erase heading not required.)

Instructions regarding War Diaries and Intelligence Summaries are contained in F. S. Regs., Part II. and the Staff Manual respectively. Title Pages will be prepared in manuscript.

Place	Date	Hour	Summary of Events and Information	Remarks and references to Appendices
BILLON WOOD	7.7.16	11.45	Enemy are retreating from CONTALMAISON LINE and his defence weakening. Batteries kept on same targets at a steady rate of fire.	
		12.50 p.m.	CONTALMAISON taken by 38 Div, who are now in S.E. corner of MAMETZ WOOD.	
		2.6	38 Div advancing. Line of batteries unchanged. During night A, C, D. fired on enemy 2nd line. 53rd Inf Bde (18 Div) relieved by 8th Inf Bde (3rd Div). 3rd Div 13th Bde take up positions for wire cutting on German 2nd line. B/83 retains new forward position for wire cutting on German position.	
CARNOY	8.7.16		B/83 except A.4 & 6.2 withdrawn from the line. A.4 & 6.2. B/83 retains new forward position of the Brigade on the line.	
" "	9.7.16		Brigade comes under 3rd Div for tactical purposes. Batteries and firing on small parties of Germans moving between BAZENTIN LE PETIT and LE GRAND WOODS.	
" "	10.7.16		Batteries bombard S. edge of BAZENTIN LE PETIT and LE GRAND WOODS. 38 Div Infantry are attacking MAMETZ WOOD. Enemy bombarded new lines on our right and left heavily during the evening. MAMETZ WOOD less 100 yds on N taken. Enemy reported to be massing for counter attack.	
" "	11.7.16		Situation quiet on our immediate front. To right and left enemy are bombarding heavily. 3rd Div Arty are cutting wire on enemy 2nd line. One battery is firing to prevent work on it or repair of wire cut.	
" "	12.7.16		Enemy artillery much more active on whole front. Batteries again fired on enemy second line. Orders received that 2nd Hun would be attacked tomorrow 14 Minuit 83rd Bde forms part of Centre Group	(4) 3rd Div. O.O. + time table and map
" "	13.7.16			

1875 Wt. W593/826 1,000,000 4/15 J.B.C. & A. A.D.S.S./Forms/C. 2118.

WAR DIARY or INTELLIGENCE SUMMARY

83rd Brigade R.F.A.

Army Form C. 2118

Place	Date	Hour	Summary of Events and Information	Remarks and references to Appendices
CARNOY	13.7.16		Enemy artillery very active. Batteries shelled enemy front line and support trenches.	
	14.7.16	3.20 a.m	Batteries opened fire on enemy front line trenches. Intense fire for 5 minutes.	
		3.25	Zero time. Infantry attack on front line.	
		4 a.m	LONGUEVAL and BAZENTIN LE PETIT on fire.	
		5 a.m	8th Brigade Inf. held up by wire.	
		6.35	8th Brigade also held up.	
		7.15	LONGUEVAL and BAZENTIN LE PETIT WOOD captured.	
		9.28	DELVILLE WOOD taken.	
		11.10	Brigade of Cavalry and 2 R.H.a Batteries have gone forward. 1B Lancers have passed on top of Battery position.	
		1 p.m	Counter attack on BAZENTIN LE GRAND.	
		2.30 p.m	8th Brigade has obtained objective and taken 200 prisoners. The left from enemy front line to support line and beyond were carried out according to programme. Enemy retaliated on infantry and on his old front line after its capture.	
THE TWINS	15.7.16		Battery advanced to new position at "A" S.26.D.7.8 "D" S.20.D.8.4 "C" S.26.B.8.8 "D" S.21.A.2.2. Bde H.Qrs. at "The Twins".	
	16.7.16		Batteries shelled HIGH WOOD, DELVILLE WOOD in support of counter attack by enemy. Nothing to report.	

WAR DIARY
or
INTELLIGENCE SUMMARY 83rd Bde R.F.A.

(Erase heading not required.)

Army Form C. 2118

Place	Date	Hour	Summary of Events and Information	Remarks and references to Appendices
THE TWINS	17/7/16		Occasional bursts of fire in support of local attack on LONGUEVAL and DELVILLE WOOD. Brigade came under orders of 9th Div	
	18/7/16		Enemy artillery very active. Apparently he has brought up a number of heavy guns. LONGUEVAL and DELVILLE WOOD were heavily bombarded by him. A hostile automatic gun of small calibre fired some thousands of rounds in the vicinity of CARNOY – MONTAUBAN road. The shell exploded with very slight sound and gave off a gas of a mixed and very peculiar odour. Our helmets and box respirators were used and no ill effects were suffered. Lee Seagrove wounded by shell fire and evacuated. Major Coltingham assumed temporary Command	
	19/7/16		All day and night the hostile artillery was very active, bombarding our front line from HIGH WOOD to DELVILLE WOOD, CATERPILLAR VALLEY, MONTAUBAN and district. A/83 had 2 casualties, from the battery was apparently observed by balloon. Our batteries kept on barrages on N and N.E of DELVILLE WOOD several times during the day on report of Germans advancing?, and at 2-35 to assist in attack on the N half of DELVILLE WOOD	
	20/7/16		Enemy artillery very active. Batteries barraged N and N.E of DELVILLE WOOD and fired bursts of fire on to FLERS – LONGUEVAL road.	
	21/7/16	11.30 a.m	Orders received from 9th Div. that the Brigade would withdraw to wagon lines	
		4.30 p.m	All batteries clear of positions. Brigade marches to BOIS de TAILLES and bivouacced	
	22/7/16	?	Brigade marches to BUSSY via CORBIE	

WAR DIARY
or
INTELLIGENCE SUMMARY 83rd Brigade R.F.a.

(Erase heading not required.)

Army Form C. 2118

Instructions regarding War Diaries and Intelligence Summaries are contained in F. S. Regs., Part II. and the Staff Manual respectively. Title Pages will be prepared in manuscript.

Place	Date	Hour	Summary of Events and Information	Remarks and references to Appendices
FONTAINE SUR SOMME	23.7.16		Brigade arrived having marched from BUSSY via AMIENS	
—	24.7.16		Nothing to report	
—	25.7.16		—	
—	26.7.16		Brigade entrained at SAINT REMY	
—	27.7.16		Brigade detrained at BAILLEUL and marched to new area. Div. H.Q. at CAESTRE, batteries at ECKE. 18 Div. now belong to 2nd Corps, 2nd Army	(5) 18 Div Cav Order No. 5
CAESTRE	28.7.16		Nothing to report	
—	29.7.16		"	
—	30.7.16		Orders received that Brigade would relieve batteries covering 3rd New Zealand Rifles Brigade. Relief to be completed by 8th and 10th August	
—	31.7.16		All guns are being overhauled by D.O.M.	

Hamer
Capt R.F.a.
Comdg 83rd Bde R.F.a.

SECRET.

COPY NO. 19

OPERATION ORDER NO. 1
- by -
Brigadier General S.F.Metcalfe, D.S.O.
Comdg. Arty., 18th Divn.

TASKS ALLOTTED TO DIVISION

(1)   The tasks allotted to the 18th Division in the forthcoming operations are :-

    (1) To secure and consolidate the line running from the Railway at A.3.c.8.6.to the junction of DUGOUT trench and BRESLAU ALLEY, thence North East up BRESLAU ALLEY to the junction of trenches at A.3.c.15.72,thence along the trench joining BRESLAU ALLEY with MINE ALLEY, thence by points 2258, 6159, POMMIERS LANE, POMMIERS REDOUBT to the junction of trenches F.6.a.70.10 and to hold them at any cost for a prolonged period against counter attack.

    (2) To consolidate the trench from MONTAUBAN through S.26.d. and c (MONTAUBAN ALLEY) and BEETLE TRENCH.

    (3) To secure and consolidate the line running from the Western corner of MONTAUBAN as far E.as Divisional Boundary, thence westwards to trench junction at S.27.c.1.7. and along trench to junction of trenches at S.26.d.7.6., thence Northwards along trench to about S.26.b.5.4. thence Westwards along the spur through S.26.a.8.3. and S.26.a.2.2. thence to join up with right of 7th Division near S.25.b.3.0. At latter point a strong point is to be constructed immediately it is gained; the 7th Division will construct 4 strong points to the west of this and to the south of the crest of the ridge, roughly along the line S.25.b.3.0. to about X.29.d.9.10 (between S.25.b. and d. and between X.30.a. and c.)

(2) DIVIDING LINE.

The 30th Division will be on our right the 7th Division of XVth Corps on our left.   The 9th Division XIII Corps in Corps Reserve.
Dividing Lines between 18th & 30th Division are shown in Map I.

(3) DIVISION FRONT.

The front allotted to the 18th Division extends from the junction of the trench at A.9.a.6.5. to a point 70 yards due east of point where CARNOY - MAMETZ road cuts trench F13/3. Total frontage 2,200 yards.

(4) OBJECTIVES.

The objectives to be attained by the 18th Division are :-

First (a) From Railway at A.3.c.8.6. to the trench connecting A.3.c.10.75 with A.2.d.75.90 - Point 35 6159 - POMMIERS REDOUBT - Junction of trenches at F.6.c.70.10.

    (b) As a support to the above and subsidiary to it, the consolidation of the following strong points :-

        (1) Junction of trenches at A.9.a.30.95.
        (2)   "   "   "   A.2.d.05.25.
        (3)   "   "   "   A.1.d.8.3.
        (4)   "   "   "   F.6.c.85.45.
        (5)   "   "   "   F.6.c.68.07.

(2)

Second. The triangle formed by the trenches at S.27.a.7.0. along MONTAUBAN ALLEY to the junction of trenches at S.26.d.6.7. along this trench to its northern extremity at S.26.b.46.40, thence to the western extremity of the trench at S.26.a.5.6. and thence to a point on the track about S.25.b.5.2.

(5) GENERAL PLAN.

The Infantry assault will take place on "Z" day, the days previous to this being known as "Y", "X", "W", "V", "U", "S", "T" &c. &c. days. The Division will attack with its three Infantry Brigades abreast. Each Brigade will place two Battalions in front line and one in support, retaining its fourth battalion in Brigade Reserve. No Divisional Reserve is kept back.
Each Brigade has one group of Field and Howitzer Batteries affiliated to it in the closest possible co-operation.

The plan adopted aims at simplifying the work of subordinate units; it is based on the idea of launching six battalions to gain the furthest objective; it provides three more battalions to fortify and garrison the nearer objective; it places in suitable localities three more battalions close up for the unexpected eventualities which every battle discloses. The whole Division will be used up unhesitatingly to gain the objectives allotted to it by superior authority, but the mere crowding of Infantry on the POMMIERS plateau will be avoided.

(6) FRONTAGES & OBJECTIVES.

Frontages and objectives allotted to Infantry Brigades (and affiliated R.F.A. Groups) are as follows :-

(a) RIGHT BRIGADE (55th).

Frontage. Junction of trench A.9/5 with BERKELEY STREET to junction of BATTY ROAD with front trench (inclu.) - 900 yards.

First Objective. From Railway at A.3.c.8.6.(exclu.) - Junction of DUGOUT trench and BRESLAU Alley - point A.2.d.8.9. to point 2250 (exclu.) - 900 yards.

Second Objective. From the road junction at the west end of MONTAUBAN(S.27.c.7.4.) along the most southerly trench running through S.27.c. thence by MONTAUBAN ALLEY to the junction of the trenches at S.26.d.6.7.

Third Objective. From the triangle formed by the trenches in the South East corner of S.27.a.(inclusive), along MONTAUBAN ALLEY as far as the trench running North at S.26.d.6.7. thence along this latter trench to its northern extremity at S.26.b.46.40.

(b) CENTRE BRIGADE (53rd)

Frontage. Junction of BATTY ROAD and front trench (exclu.) - ~~650 yards.~~ to junction of YORK Road and trench A 7/2 (inclu.) - 650 yards.

First Objective. Point 2258 (inclusive) - POMMIERS TRENCH as its junction with POPOFF Lane (inclu.) - 650 yards.

Second Objective. From the junction of trenches at S.26.d.6.7., along MONTAUBAN ALLEY as far as its junction with the MONTAUBAN-HAMETZ Road (inclu.)

(3).

Third Objective. From the northern end of the trench running from N.W. to S.E. through S.26.b.(S.26.b.46.40) (exclusive) to the western extremity of the trench running from S.26.a.88.45 to S.26.a.50.60(inclu.)

(c) **LEFT BRIGADE (54th).**

Frontage. Junction of YORK ROAD and trench A.7/2 (exclu.) to a point 70 yards due east of point where MAMETZ-CARNOY Road cuts through trench F.12/3 - 700 yards.

First Objective. Junction of POMMIERS Trench and POPOFF Lane (exclu.) - POMMIERS TRENCH to its junction with BLACK ALLEY (inclu.).

Second Objective. POMMIERS REDOUBT and the trench to the west of it as far as its junction with BEETLE ALLEY.

Third Objective. From the western extremity of the trench running from S.26.a.88.45 to S.26.a.50.60(exclu.) to the junction between the XIIIth and XVth Corps about S.26.b.5.2.

(7) **TASKS.**

The main tasks of the Infantry will be :-

(a) **RIGHT BRIGADE.**

(1) To secure and consolidate the trench given as its nearer objective in para.6(a) and assist by flanking fire from Machine Guns the attack on the GLATZ Redoubt by the 30th Div.

(2) Two platoons, under a selected officer will be detailed by the Brigade Commander to deal with the craters and the maze of small trenches immediately north of them, in order that the general advance of the Brigade may not be delayed.

(3) On reaching its second objective to establish a strong point in the houses near the road junction at the West end of MONTAUBAN and consolidate that part of MONTAUBAN ALLEY allotted to it on para.6(a).

(4) On reaching its third objective to -
 (a) consolidate the trenches existing on it
 (b) place machine guns in the trench running from N.W. to S.E. through S.26.b. in such positions as will enable them to deal with any threatened counter-attack from the direction of the valley N.& N.E.of MONTAUBAN.

(b) **CENTRE BRIGADE.**

(1) To consolidate and hold the trench allotted to it as its first objective in para.6(b).

(2) To assist the Left Brigade in its attack on the POMMIERS REDOUBT; mutual arrangements for this to be made beforehand between Brigadiers CENTRE and LEFT Brigade.

(3) To consolidate that portion of MONTAUBAN ALLEY from the junction of trenches S.26.d.6.7 to S.26.c.33.45 and to join up from this point with the right of the 54th Brigade in BEETLE ALLEY.

(4)

(2)

SECRET

(4).

  (4). On reaching its third objective, firstly to construct strong points making use of the existing trenches and secondly to dig new fire trenches where necessary to make the line continuous.

  (5) To prevent enemy removing guns from CATERPILLAR VALLEY.

 (c) LEFT BRIGADE.

  (1) To secure BLACK ALLEY and the part of POMMIERS Trench allotted to it.

  (2) From these positions to organise and carry out an attack on the POMMIERS REDOUBT.

  (3) To secure and consolidate that portion of BEETLE TRENCH between S.25.d.98.27 and its junction with the MONTAUBAN-MAMETZ Road.

  (4) On reaching its third objective to dig new fire trenches where necessary to join the left of the Centre Brigade and the right of the XVth Corps.

  (5) To send forward LEWIS Guns to overlook the CATERPILLAR Valley and the valley East of MAMETZ WOOD and prevent guns being removed.

(d) Leading troops of all three Brigades on reaching their third objective will send forward detachments with machine guns to cover the work of consolidation, establish observation posts overlooking CATERPILLAR WOOD Valley and prevent the withdrawal of hostile batteries from that neighbourhood. They will be supported by Field Guns.

(e) The line Railway at A.3.c.8.6. – trench junction at A.2.d.8.9. – Point 2258 – POMMIERS trench to its junction with BLACK ALLEY, will be held at all costs against counter attacks, even if MONTAUBAN and MAMETZ should not be captured.

(f) Troops will be specially told off by each Brigade to "clean up" hostile trenches and deal with any of the enemy remaining there after the leading troops have passed over them.

(8) STRONG POINTS.

  To carry out the above tasks definite infantry units will be detailed to occupy and prepare for "all round defence" certain specified localities in the hostile lines as strong points. These points are shown in Map I.

(9) ARTILLERY SUPPORT.

  The Infantry attack will be supported by ~~18th Divl. Artillery.~~
  18th Divisional Artillery.
  Two ~~22nd~~ Brigades of 9th Div. Arty. (less one 4.5" How. Batt.)
  XIII Corps H.A.
  Trench Mortar Batteries of 18th Division & 9th Div.

(5).

(10). GROUPING OF ARTILLERY.

The batteries of Divisional Artillery (and attached batteries) will form three Groups. Each Group will support the attack of one Infantry Brigade as under:-

Right Group - O.C.Lt.-Col.Blois,D.S.O. - 55th Inf. Bde.
Centre Group - " " Lt.-Col.Seagran. - 53rd Inf. Bde.
Left Group - " " Lt.-Col.Thorp. - 54th Inf. Bde.

Each Group will be responsible for the ground to be covered by its affiliated Inf. Bde., and will be capable of reinforcing neighbouring groups should occasion arise.

The 2" Medium Trench Mortar Batteries (and one 240 mm Trench Mortar, if available) will be grouped under the Divisional Trench Mortar Officer, who will be situated in CARNOY, and in communication with 18th Divisional Artillery, through Left Group forward exchange.

(11) ARTILLERY BOMBARDMENT.

Will consist of :-

(a) A five days ("U" to "Y" day) preliminary bombardment of german defences, with a concentrated bombardment of 65 minutes previous to the assault on the 6th day ("Z" day).

(b) An Artillery bombardment, carried out in a succession of lifts to support the assault.

(c) An Artillery barrage against all counter attacks during consolidation of position gained.

(12) PRELIMINARY BOMBARDMENT.

During preliminary bombardment the following tasks will be undertaken :-

(a) Destruction of enemy's wire by 18-pr. & 2" trench mortars.

(b) Destruction of observation stations, communication trenches, machine gun gun emplacements, etc., by 4.5" Hows., assisted by 2" Trench Mortars on front system of trenches.

(c) Destruction of hostile system of trenches by XIII Corps H.A.

(d) Bombardment of billets by XIII Corps H.A.

(e) Counter Battery work by XIII Corps H.A.

(f) Shelling of all approaches and communications by day and night with a view of preventing replenishing of ammunition, food, water, etc., by XIII Corps H.A., 18-prs. & 4.5" Hows.

(g) Preventing repair of wire and trenches by night, by 18-prs. & 4.5" Hows., assisted by machine guns and rifle fire.

(h) Concentration of fire on portion of the defences.

(i) Shrapnel barrage in support of gas discharge.

Appendix 'A' "Programme of Preliminary Bombardment" forwarded herewith indicates tasks to be undertaken on each day and night respectively.

This programme is intended as a general guide to Group Commanders, circumstances may necessitate the hours and tasks being somewhat changed, these should however be adhered to as far as is possible.

(13) DESTRUCTION OF ENEMY'S WIRE.

Five batteries per group have been detailed for wire cutting. Each of these batteries has been assigned a definite strip of german defences, and is responsible for cutting all wire within this strip, and preventing repair at night.
(N.B. These strips are identical with the strips allotted to these same batteries during the bombardment to support the assault and are shown on diagram in Appendix 'B'.)

The wire on the succeeding lines of trenches will be engaged in accordance with "Preliminary Instructions in wire cutting issued to all concerned.

The wire on the front line (and support line, where it is sufficiently close) will be engaged by the 2" Medium Trench Mortar Batteries as shown in Appendix 'B'.

The wire in front of POMMIERS REDOUBT and on the western side of LOOP TRENCH will be engaged by the forward batteries in CARNOY valley on 'Z' day in accordance with Appendix 'B' as well as by the Left Group wire cutting batteries during previous bombardment.

Group Commanders, and the Divisional Trench Mortar Officer will keep in constant touch with Infantry Brigade Commanders to obtain all possible information from reports of Infantry Patrols sent forward to ascertain damage to wire.

(14) BOMBARDMENT TO SUPPORT ASSAULT.

The bombardment to support the assault will consist of a concentrated bombardment from - 65 to zero hour, followed by a succession of lifts timed to conform with Corps Artillery lifts and the forward movement of the attacking infantry.

The Corps Artillery and Divisional Artillery lifts are shown on Map I. The times shown at right end of lines refer to Corps Artillery, those at the left end of the lines refer to Divisional Artillery. These lines indicate that at the hours stipulated no Corps Artillery or Divnl. Artillery respectively will be firing South of these lines.

(7)

As an indication to the attacking infantry that a lift is about to occur all 18-pr. batteries will fire H.E. exclusively for 30 seconds before each lift, namely about 5 rounds per gun.

Group Commanders will impress on all battery commanders that it is essential that there should be no pause or cessation of fire as each lift occurs; batteries will continue firing at the same rate of fire, the "lift" being effected by the necessary increase of range only.

Five 18-pr. batteries per group will be detailed to cover the assault, each battery being allotted a strip of german defences as shown in Appendix 'B'.

The batteries of the 51st Brigade, R.F.A., situated in CARNOY valley are allotted special tasks and will be employed for meeting any unforseen eventualities.

The three 4.5" Howr. batteries of 18th Divisional Arty. when not employed for counter battery work with gas shell by XIII Corps H.A., will engage portions of german trenches in rear of 18-pr. barrage from which fire might be brought to bear on assaulting infantry.

During the assault concentration of fire will be carried out on the POMMIERS Redoubt, and on western portion of MONTAUBAN village.

Full particulars and time table for "Bombardment to Support Assault" are contained in Appendix 'B'.

(15) ARTILLERY BARRAGE DURING CONSOLIDATION OF POSITION.

Should it be necessary at any time to establish a barrage to repel a counter attack or assist our infantry in consolidating a position gained, the barrage front of each wire cutting battery will be represented by the width of the strip allotted to it as this point.

(16) DEFENCE OF THE FRONT.

During the whole period of the Preliminary Bombardment Group Commanders will be responsible for the defence of the front allotted to them, the 5 wire cutting batteries being employed to establish any necessary barrage to check an attack or prevent a raid.

(17) TRENCH MORTARS.

Instructions and tasks for Medium and Heavy Trench Mortars are contained in Appendix 'E'. A copy of these instructions has been issued to the Officer Commanding each trench mortar battery.

(18) COMMUNICATIONS.

(a) Telephone. These have been duplicated and triplicated wherever possible, and buried at the bottom of communication trenches or else placed in separate trenches 6 feet deep.

On each Brigade front 4 pairs of wires have been run forward from Observation Stations to points close to the front line. These lines will be used in the first place for forward observation during wire cutting, and secondly to form advanced terminals for any forward wires required by Liason Officers and Observation Officers detailed to proceed beyond German front line trench.

(5)

(b) Wireless. An advanced wireless station will be established by the Divisional Signal Company at A.19.a.5.0. This station will be in communication with the main wireless station at Divisional Headquarters.
   Trench Sets. There will be one wireless set which will move forward with the attacking troops. Its position will be determined by the Divisional Signal Company.

(c) VISUAL. Divisional Signal Company will establish signalling stations at 3 Brigade Headquarters and at A.13.d.1.1.
   In addition to the above Group Commanders will establish every possible means of visual signalling between Observation Stations and batteries, and will select certain Observation Stations to act as receiving stations for signals sent back by F.O.O's or Liason Officer after the advance. Suitable sites within the german defences will be selected previously for signalling back from.
   All F.O.O's and Liason Officers sent forward will be instructed as to which Observation Stations have been selected for receiving messages and should make certain that they know the exact position of these stations, and can identify them by looking back from our forward trenches.

(19) DISTINGUISHING MARKS.

The following distinguishing marks will be employed to enable the Artillery to follow the movements of the Infantry in the attack :-

(a) Flags, red and yellow halved diagonally. 1 per platoon and 1 per Company Headquarters.

(b) Tin discs, painted white. They will be carried in the centre of the back suspended by a string round the neck with another string tied to the belt to keep them in place when the men lie down.

(20) GAS.

Arrangements have been made for a limited instalment of gas in suitable places along the front.
The discharge of the gas will be supported by heavy shrapnel fire, as shown in Appendix 'A'.

(21) AMMUNITION.

Appendix 'C' forwarded herewith gives "Approximate Allotment of Ammunition for various tasks per gun". This table has been worked out on the basis of a wire cutting battery, consequently the expenditure shown is greater than the average expenditure per gun including forward batteries.
This table is intended as a guide to Group Commanders in allotting number of rounds to various tasks, and in ensuring that sufficient ammunition is brought up to the guns to allow of subsequent tasks being carried out.
No gas shells will be fired by 4.5" Howrs. previous to -65 time on zero day.

(9)

(22) RATE OF FIRE.

18-pr. Normal rate for ordinary bombardment will be 1 round per gun per minute.

Intense fire - 3 rounds per gun per minute.

4.5"How. Normal 1 round per gun per 2 minutes.

Intense 2 rounds per gun per minute.

For special cases such as counter attack by the enemy the rate of fire is left to the discretion of the Artillery Commander on the spot who must be the best judge of the situation.

(23) COMMUNICATION WITH AEROPLANES.

XIIIth Corps Contact Patrol Aeroplanes will be distinguished by a broad black band under both lower planes and by streamers from the ends of both planes.
The firing of a white VERY light by the aeroplane will mean "I am ready to receive a message".
The attacking infantry will signal to aeroplanes by means of
(1) Flares.
(2) Mirrors.
Flares and mirrors will mean "I am here and, so far as I know, within 50 yards of the actual firing line".
These flares and mirrors will only be used when the leading infantry have either
(a) reached their first, second or third objective
(b) have been prevented from reaching any of their objectives.
Messages to aeroplanes from Battalion and Brigade Headquarters will be sent by means of either lamps or panel shutters.

(24) FORWARD OBSERVING OFFICERS & LIASON OFFICERS.

Each Group will detail 2 officers to act as Liason Officers with two battalions of the Brigade they support.
In addition 2 Forward Observing Officers will be detailed by each Group to follow the infantry advance, and endeavour to establish forward observation stations.
The party and equipment to accompany these officers will be in accordance with instructions previously issued.

(25) COOLING OF GUNS DURING BOMBARDMENT.

Attention is drawn to "Notes on Care of Guns during prolonged Bombardments" O.B./1717.

(26) SPARE PARTS.

Spare parts for guns will be disposed of in accordance with previous instructions issued.

(27) PREPARATION FOR FORWARD MOVE.

Certain batteries and guns will be held in readiness to move to forward positions in accordance with instructions contained in Appendix 'D'.

(10)

(28) THIS Operation Order is on no account to be taken further forward than Battery Positions.

(29) APPENDICES & MAPS

The following Appendices and Maps are forwarded herewith :-

    Appendix 'A'. Time Table of Preliminary Bombardment.
    " 'B'. " " " Bombardment to Support Assault.
    " 'C'. " " " Approximate allotment of Ammunition to various tasks.
    " 'D'. " " " Preparation for Forward Advance.
    " 'E'. " " " Trench Mortar Batteries.
    Map I. Indicating Divisional Boundaries, Group Boundaries, and Artillery Lifts.

(30) PLEASE ACKNOWLEDGE.

[signature]

Captain, R.A.,
Brigade Major, R.A., 18th Division.

H.Q., R.A., 18/Div.
19th June, 1916.

Copies to :-

    XIII Corps, R.A.   -   No. 1.
    18th Division.   -   No. 2.
    7th Division.   -   No. 3.
    30th Division.   -   No. 4.
    9th Divisional Arty. -   No. 5.
    53rd Infantry Bde.   -   No. 6.
    54th   "   "   -   No. 7.
    55th   "   "   -   No. 8.
    9th Squadron, R.F.C. -   No. 9.
    Right Group, R.A.   -   Nos. 10-18.
    Centre Group, R.A.   -   " 19-26.
    Left Group, R.A.   -   " 27-35.
    XIII Corps, H.A.   -   No. 36.

APPENDIX "A".

PROGRAMME OF PRELIMINARY BOMBARDMENT.

(1)   The attached programme is worked out with a view to conforming with instructions issued as regards sequence of the bombardment, and to minimise the difficulties of observation caused by smoke and dust of one battery interfering with another.

(2)   SPECIAL HOURS ALLOTTED TO BATTERIES.

    Special hours have been allotted to the various batteries concerned for engaging the front system of trenches, this does not preclude other batteries from engaging trenches further to the rear at these times provided the targets engaged are not obscured by the guns firing on trenches in advance.

(3)   WIRE CUTTING.

    Wire cutting will be carried out in accordance with previous instructions issued. Group Commanders will issue necessary instructions within their Group to prevent the wire cutting batteries interfering with each other.

(4)   PREVENTING REPAIR OF WIRE & TRENCHES.

    Each 18-pr. battery will be responsible for the front allotted to it for wire cutting, as regards prevention of repairs at night. Table 'C' indicates approximate allowance of ammunition for this task, this ammunition should be expended in irregular bursts of fire throughout the night under instructions to be issued by Group Commanders.

(5)   SHELLING OF APPROACHES & COMMUNICATIONS.

    The shelling of approaches and communications will be allotted to Groups as under :-

Right Group
- (18-prs. Western exits of MONTAUBAN.
- Tracks from CATERPILLAR WOOD to MONTAUBAN.
- (4.5"How. Communication trenches & Trench junctions in A.3.a.

Centre Group
- (18-prs. CATERPILLAR WOOD Valley, and MONTAUBAN - MAMETZ Road.
- (4.5"How: LOOP TRENCH, MINE ALLEY, & POPOFF LANE.

Left Group
- (18-prs. Junction of valleys and trenches in S.20.c.
- (4.5"How: BLACK ALLEY and MONTAUBAN ALLEY.

    Group Commanders will detail at least two 18-pr. batteries and one 4.5" howitzer per night for the shelling of approaches. These batteries will have to carry out this task in addition to preventing repair of wire on the portion of front allotted to them.

    The shelling of approaches by 18-prs. will consist of approximately 12 salvoes per hour fired at irregular intervals and changed localities throughout the night.

The night

(2) (Appendix "A" contd.)

The night should be considered as lasting from 8 P.M. to 5 A.M.
4.5" Hows: will fire approximately 6 rounds per hour at the communication trenches.
The shelling of Communications and Approaches in rear will be carried out at irregular intervals throughout the day.

(6) TEST CONCENTRATION OF FIRE.

Tests of concentration of fire will be carried out by Groups in accordance with attached Programme. These concentrations will consist of a test carried out by Groups on various portions of the front.
Batteries will fire consecutively at 10 minutes interval, and effect of fire will be observed.
Forward batteries will remain silent during these concentrations.

(7) SHRAPNEL BARRAGE IN SUPPORT OF DISCHARGE OF GAS.

Should the wind be favourable it is intended on one of the nights previous to assault to discharge a gas cloud with a view to inflicting loss on the enemy by taking them by surprise.
Notification of such a discharge will be forwarded to Groups previously. - The five wire cutting batteries per Group will support the discharge of gas by establishing a heavy shrapnel barrage, at the rate of 3 rounds per 18-pr. per minute for two periods of 8 minutes.
This barrage will be carried out with the following lifts:-

  Gas discharge begins:-   0.00 time.
  Barrage front trench:-   0.30 to 0.32 and 1.15 to 1.20.
  Lift to second line :-   0.32 to 0.37 " 1.20 to 1.23.
  Return to front line:-   0.37 to 0.40 " 1.23 to 1.25.

(8) TIMES RESERVED FOR CORPS ARTILLERY.

Certain periods daily have been reserved for Corps Artillery for bombardment of front trenches, this is to ensure the Divisional Artillery and Corps Artillery not interfering with each others' tasks.
Copies of diagram indicating wire to be engaged daily by 18-prs. have been forwarded to XIII Corps H.A. who will refrain from firing on these trenches at the hours detailed for 18-pr. wire cutting.

(9) TRENCH MORTARS.

Special hours have been allotted to Medium Trench Mortar batteries for wire cutting. These batteries will refrain from firing at the front trench during the other hours of the day.

(10) DESTRUCTION OF OBSERVATION STATIONS, MACHINE GUNS, COMMUNICATION TRENCHES, ETC., BY 4.5" HOWS:

Special hours have not been allotted for 4.5" How: firing on front trenches - Group Commanders will allot tasks to their 4.5" How: batteries within their own fronts, and regulate their fire so as not to interfere with wire cutting operations.

(11) GAS SHELLS.

(Appendix "A" contd.)

(11) GAS SHELLS.

The use of the Divisional 4.5" How: batteries will be required by XIII Corps H.A. from 5 minutes previous to zero hour for counter battering work with gas shell - It is not certain yet how long these guns will be required for this task.

(12) FORWARD BATTERIES.

The forward batteries (51st Brigade, R.F.A.) in the CARNOY valley will not take part in the preliminary bombardment, and will be kept as silent as possible. Group Commanders should however endeavour to carry out any possible registration of these batteries which they consider could be done without disclosing their positions.

The objectives requiring special registration may be obtained from the tasks allotted to these batteries in Appendix "B".

(13) TESTS OF FORWARD BARRAGE NEAR CATERPILLAR WOOD.

It is hoped to carry out two tests during the preliminary bombardment of the final barrage required after the assault.

This test will be carried out by all 15 wire cutting batteries firing salvoes at 4 minutes interval commencing with the most easterly barrage battery of the Right Group. Full particulars of the test will be forwarded to Group Commanders and to O.C. 9th Squadron, R.F.C.

(5)　　　　　　　　　　　　　　(Appendix 'A' contd.)

"W" DAY.

TIME	NATURE OF GUN.	TASK.
10 AM to 1 PM) 4 PM to 8 PM)	18-prs:	Wire cutting on POMMIERS TRENCH line in accordance with Programme. Batteries may continue from 1 to 3 PM provided observation is not obscured by 2" T.M.
3 PM.	18-prs:	Test forward barrage near CATERPILLAR WOOD with aeroplane observation.
Irregular intervals.	18-prs: & 4.5" Hows:	Approaches and communications.
All day.	4.5" Hows:	Same as "V" day.
5 AM to 7 AM) 1 PM to 4 PM)	2" T.M.	Wire cutting front and support trenches.
9 AM to 10 AM.	18-prs: & 4.5" Hows:	Concentration of Left Group wire cutting batteries on POMMIERS Redoubt.
7 AM to 10 AM.	XIII Corps HA	Reserved for Corps Artillery on front trenches.
W/X Night.	18prs: & 4.5" Hows:	Same as V/W Night.

"X" DAY.

TIME	NATURE OF GUN.	TASK.
10 AM to 4 PM.	18-prs:	Wire cutting front and support trenches in accordance with wire cutting instructions.
Irregular intervals.	18-prs: & 4.5" Hows:	Approaches and communications.
All Day.	4.5" Hows:	Same as "W" day.
6 AM to 10 AM) 6 PM to 8 PM)	2" T.M.	Destruction of trenches and wire cutting.
6 PM to 7 PM.	18-prs: & 4.5" Hows:	Concentration of centre wire cutting battery from each group on MONTAUBAN commencing with Right Group battery, 10 minutes interval between batteries.
9 AM to 10 AM) 4 PM to 6 PM)	XIII Corps HA	Reserved for Corps H.A. on front trenches.
X/Y Night.	18-prs: & 4.5" Hows:	Same as W/X night.

(4) (Appendix 'A' contd.)

"U" DAY.

TIME.	NATURE OF GUN.	TASK.
All day.	18-prs:	Wire cutting in Second Line in accordance with Wire Cutting Programme. Registration if required.
" "	4.5"Hows:	Complete Registration.
" "	2" T.M.	Remain silent.
" "	240 mm T.M.	"
U/V Night.	18-prs:	Communications, approaches and preventing repair of wire.
" "	4.5"Hows:	Communication trenches.

"V" DAY.

TIME.	NATURE OF GUN.	TASK.
6 AM to 9 AM) 12.30 to 3PM)	18-prs:	Wire cutting on Third line in accordance with wire cutting instructions. Batteries may continue firing up to 11 AM provided observation is not obscured by 2" T.Ms.
4 P.M.	18-prs:	Test forward barrage near CATERPILLAR WOOD with aeroplane observation.
All day.	4.5"Hows:	O.Ps, Machine gun emplacements and communication trenches.
9 AM to 11AM) 5 PM to 6 PM)	2" T.Ms.	Wire cutting front and support trenches.
11AM to12.30PM) 3 PM to 5 PM)	XIII Corps H.A.	Reserved for Corps H.A. on front trenches.
4PM to 4.20PM	18-prs.	Concentration of Right Group wire cutting batteries on MONTAUBAN.
V/W Night.	18-prs & 4.5" Hows:	Same as U/V Night. 18-prs. ready to support gas barrage if necessary.

(Appendix 'A' contd.)

"Y" DAY.

TIME.	NATURE OF GUN.	TASK.
11 AM to 1 PM	18-prs:	Wire cutting on any portion of wire left uncut. Batteries may continue from 1 PM to 3 PM provided 2" T.M. do not interfere.
4.30 PM to 8 PM		Approaches and communications at irregular intervals.
All day.	4.5"Hows:	Same as "X" day.
6 AM to 9 AM. 1 PM to 3 PM.	2" T.M.	Destruction of trenches and wire.
9 AM to 11 AM. 3 PM to 4.20 PM.	XIII Corps, H.A.	Reserved for Corps Artillery on front trenches.
6 AM to 7.20 AM.	18-prs: & 4.5" Hows:	Concentration of Centre Group batteries on the LOOP.
Y/Z Night.	18-prs: & 4.5" Hows:	Same as X/Y Night.

"Z" DAY.

In accordance with Bombardment to Support Assault, Appendix "B".

7.15 a.m - 7.20 a.m. Intense fire in support of smoke

APPENDIX "B".

BOMBARDMENT TO SUPPORT ASSAULT.

(1) PHASES.

The bombardment to support the assault will be divided into distinctive phases, as under.

[margin: 1 July]

6.25 to 7.30	Phase I.	From 65 minutes previous to zero time up to zero time. Intense final bombardment preparatory to assault.
7.30 - 7.34	Phase II.	From 0.00 to 0.04 minutes. Bombardment of line "B" for 4 minutes.
7.34 - 7.39	Phase III.	From 0.04 to 0.09 minutes. Bombardment of line "C" for 5 minutes.
7.39 - 7.49	Phase IV.	From 0.09 to 0.19 minutes. Bombardment of line "D" for 10 minutes.
7.49 - 8.28	Phase V.	From 0.19 to 0.58 minutes. Bombardment of line "E" by Left Group and one battery of Centre Group. LOOP TRENCH, BLIND ALLEY by Centre Group. Concentration on MONTAUBAN, THE TWINS, THE MILL and communication trenches by Right Group.
8.28 to 9.30	Phase VI.	From 0.58 to 2.00 minutes. Two minute test barrage on line "H". Concentration of Right Group batteries and forward batteries on MONTAUBAN. Shelling of BEETLE ALLEY, MONTAUBAN ALLEY, THE TWINS, BLIND ALLEY, THE LOOP, etc.
9.30 to 10	Phase VII.	2.00 to 2.30 minutes. Shrapnel barrage starting from "F" line and moving in front of infantry by increments of range, until final barrage is established on line "H".
10 a.m.	Phase VIII.	2.30 onwards protection of infantry during consolidation of position gained.

(2) TIME TABLE.

Time Table of bombardment with actual tasks allotted to each battery in the various phases is attached.

(3) CHART.

The attached chart indicates trenches to be engaged by each of the 5 wire cutting batteries per group during the advance.

The lines have been lettered in accordance with preliminary instructions already issued.

(4) 4.5" Howitzer BATTERIES.

When not engaged in Counter Battery work with gas shell these batteries will engage trenches somewhat in rear of front barrage in accordance with time table, and on special points to be selected by Group Commanders.

(2)　　　　　　　　　　　　　　　　　(Appendix "B" contd.)

(5) **FORWARD BATTERIES.**

These will be employed for dealing with any unforseen contingencies, and will be allotted certain tasks for which they are well suited owing to their close range.

(6) **SHRAPNEL & H.E.**

During the bombardment 18-pr. batteries will fire shrapnel with a mixture of 20% H.E.

As an indication to the infantry that a lift is about to occur, all 18-pr. batteries will fire exclusively H.E. ammunition for 30 seconds at an increased pace previous to each lift, namely about 5 rounds per gun.

All concentrations on MONTAUBAN should consist mostly of H.E. ammunition, a proportion of this class of ammunition should consequently be reserved for these tasks.

(7) **FLANK BARRAGES.**

Throughout the advance Group Commanders will hold themselves in readiness for the possibility of having to establish a flank barrage to protect a salient that may be formed owing to some portion of the advance being temporarily checked.

(3).   (Appendix "B" contd.)

PHASE I.

35 minutes previous to zero time up to zero time.   6.25 — 7.30

BATTERY.	OBJECTIVE.	REMARKS.
15 wire cutting batteries	Line "A".	Intense fire.
D/82, D/83, D/84.	Communication trenches & trench junctions on respective fronts, up to 5 minutes before zero time.	Under instructions to be issued by Group Commanders. Counter battery work under XIII Corps H.A. for 5 minutes previous to zero time.
Forward Batteries :- A/51. B/51	Remain silent. Wire in front of POMMIERS REDOUBT.	During last 15 minutes.
C/51 (A.15.d.7.9. (F.17.b.2.2. (F.12.c.7.3.	Enfilade BAY TRENCH. " BLACK ALLEY. " MONTAUBAN main street.	" " " " " " " " "
D/51.	BUND TRENCH from BAY LANE to TRIANGLE.	" " " "
2" T.Ms.	Front & Support trench.	
Heavy T.Ms.	Trench junction in rear of CRATERS.	

PHASE II. — 0.00 to 0.04.   7.30 — 7.34

15 wire cutting batteries.	Line "B".	Intense fire.
D/82, D/83, D/84.	Counter battery work.	Under orders of XIII Corps H.A. with gas shell.
Forward Batteries:- A/51.	Enfilade MINE ALLEY & BRESLAU ALLEY.	
B/51.	Same as Phase I.	
C/51 (A.15.d. (F.17.b. (F.12.c.	Enfilade BUND TRENCH. " BLACK ALLEY. Same as Phase I.	
D/51.	POMMIERS TRENCH.	100 yards either side of junction with POMMIERS LANE.

(Appendix "B" contd.)

(4).

PHASE III. - 0.04 to 0.09.

BATTERY.	OBJECTIVE.	REMARKS.
15 wire cutting batteries.	Line "C".	7.34 — 7.39
D/82, D/83, D/84.	Same as Phase II.	
Forward Batteries:-		
A/51.	Same as Phase II.	
B/51.	Same as Phase II.	
C/51 (A.15.d. (F.17.b. (F.12.c.	Enfilade BUND SUPPORT. " BLACK ALLEY. Same as Phase I.	Only North of Line "C".
D/51.	Same as Phase II.	

PHASE IV. - 0.09 to 0.19.   7.39 — 7.49

BATTERY	OBJECTIVE	REMARKS
15 wire cutting batteries.	Line "D".	
D/82, D/83, D/84.	BEETLE ALLEY & MONTAUBAN ALLEY.	On their respective Group fronts, as soon as Counter Battery Work is finished.
Forward batteries :-		
A/51.	Same as Phase II.	
B/51.	Enfilade LOOP Trench.	
C/51 (A.15.d. (F.17.b. (F.12.c.	" POMMIERS LANE. " BLACK ALLEY. Remain silent.	Only North of Line "D".
D/51.	POMMIERS Redoubt.	

(Appendix "B" contd.)

(5).

PHASE V. - 0.19 to 0.58   7.49 — 8.28

BATTERY.	OBJECTIVE.	REMARKS.
Left Group Wire Cutting Batteries and B/83.	Line "E".	Normal rate of fire intense fire last 10 minutes.
Centre Group Wire Cutting Batteries.	LOOP TRENCH, BLIND ALLEY, ETC.	" " " "
Right Group Wire Cutting Batteries.	Concentration on Western extremity of MONTAUBAN.	Normal rate of fire, bursts of intense fire, mostly H.E.
D/82.	POMMIERS REDOUBT.	Steady rate of fire.
D/83.	THE TWINS.	" " " "
D/84.	MONTAUBAN MILL.	" " " "
Forward Batteries:-		
A/51.	Same as Phase II.	Only North of Line "D".
B/51.	Western extremity of MONTAUBAN.	
C/51 (A.15.d.	Bursts of fire at S.20.c.2.8.	On tracks at junction of valleys.
(F.17.b.	" " " "	" " "
(F.12.c.	Same as Phase I.	
D/51.	POMMIERS REDOUBT.	Steady rate of fire.

PHASE VI. - 0.58 to 2.00.   8.28 — 9.30

15 Wire Cutting Batteries.	2 minutes test barrage on Line "H".	From 1.00 to 1.02. Intense fire. Barrage will be observed by aeroplane and corrections dropped by message at Divnl. Arty. H.Q. and passed to Groups.
Left Group wire cutting batteries.	BENTLE TRENCH.	Steady rate of fire.
Centre Group wire cutting batteries.	MONTAUBAN ALLEY, BLIND ALLEY & LOOP TRENCH.	" " " "
Right Group wire cutting batteries.	Concentration on Western portion of MONTAUBAN.	Bursts of fire.
D/82.	MONTAUBAN.	" " "
D/83.	"	" " "
D/84.	THE TWINS.	" " "
Forward batteries.		
A/51.	Same as Phase II.	Steady rate of fire.
B/51.	Western extremity of MONTAUBAN.	Bursts of fire.
C/51 (A.15.d.	Same as Phase V.	
(F.17.b.	MONTAUBAN.	Steady rate of fire.
(F.12.c.	"	" " "
D/51.	MONTAUBAN.	" " "

(Appendix "B" contd.)

(6).

PHASE VII. - 2.00 to 2.30.   9.30 - 10

BATTERY.	OBJECTIVE.	REMARKS.
15 wire cutting batteries.	Barrage to be on line "F" for 5 minutes previous to 2.00. At 2.00 the barrage will lift by increments of range of 50 yards until line "H" is reached at 2.30	The distance from line "F" to line "H" is approximately 1000 yards for all batteries-Batteries will consequently open the barrage at a range 1000 yards short of range required for barrage "H" & will increase their range at the rate of 50 yards every 1½ minutes.
D/82, D/83, D/84. Forward batteries.	CATERPILLAR WOOD.	On their respective Group fronts.
A/51.	" "	On Centre Group front, sweeping. Moderate rate of fire.
B/51.	" "	On Right Group front, sweeping. Moderate rate of fire.
C/51.	" "	On Left Group front, all four guns. Moderate rate of fire.
D/51.	" "	On Centre Group front.

PHASE VIII. - 2.30 onwards.   10 a.m

Wire cutting batteries.	Barrage "H".	Steady rate of fire, periodic bursts and ready to turn on intense bombardment if required.
Remainder.	Same as Phase VII.	

SECRET.

NO. 2
AMENDMENTS TO 18TH DIVNL. ARTY. OPERATION ORDER NO. 1.

Appendix "B", Phase VII & VIII should be amended as under.

Phase VII - 2.00 to 2.30

BATTERY.	OBJECTIVE.	REMARKS.
15 Wire Cutting Batteries.	Barrage to be on line "F" for 5 minutes previous to 2.00. At 2.00 the barrage will lift by increments of range of 50 yards until line "H" is reached at 2.30.	The distance from line "F" to line "H" is approximately 1000 yards for all batteries. Batteries will consequently open the barrage at a range 1000 yards short of range required for barrage "H" and will increase their range by increments of 50 yds. every 1½ minutes. The four right batteries of Right Group (C/85, A/50, C/84, A/84) will increase their range at a slower rate, 50 yds. every 2½ minutes until line "H" is reached.
D/82, D/83, D/84.	Western houses of MONTAUBAN.	Bursts of fire up to 2.15, intense from 2.15 onwards. Lift off MONTAUBAN at 2.25.
A/51.	MARLBORO WOOD.	
B/51.	Western corner of MONTAUBAN.	Orchards & houses just east of Right Group boundary.
C/51.	CATERPILLAR WOOD.	MARICOURT Section to enfilade western portion of wood.
D/51.	CATERPILLAR WOOD.	On Centre Group Front.

PHASE VIII. - 2.30 onwards.

Wire Cutting Batteries.	Barrage "H".	Steady rate of fire, periodic bursts of fire, and ready to turn on intense fire if necessary.
D/82, D/83, D/84.	CATERPILLAR WOOD on respective Group fronts.	During this phase forward observation must be obtained as soon as possible, and barrage regulated by actual observation and reports from Liason Officer.
A/51.	-do-	
B/51.	-do-	
C/51.	-do-	
D/51.	MARLBORO WOOD.	

(signed) C.A. Brooke
Captain, R.A.,
Brigade Major, R.A., 18th Division.

H.Q., R.A., 18/Div.
27th June, 1916.

Copies to all concerned.

SECRET.

NO. 2
AMENDMENTS TO 18TH DIVNL. ARTY. OPERATION ORDER NO. 1.

Appendix "B", Phase <u>VII</u> & <u>VIII</u> should be amended as under.

Phase <u>VII</u> - 2.00 to 2.30

BATTERY.	OBJECTIVE.	REMARKS.
15 Wire Cutting Batteries.	Barrage to be on line "F" for 5 minutes previous to 2.00. At 2.00 the barrage will lift by increments of range of 50 yards until line "H" is reached at 2.30.	The distance from line "F" to line "H" is approximately 1000 yards for all batteries.- Batteries will consequently open the barrage at a range 1000 yards short of range required for barrage "H" and will increase their range by increments of 50 yds. every 1½ minutes. The four right batteries of Right Group (C/85, A/50, C/84, A/84) will increase their range at a slower rate, 50 yds. every 2½ minutes until line "H" is reached.
D/82, D/83, D/84.	Western houses of MONTAUBAN.	Bursts of fire up to 2.15, intense from 2.15 onwards. Lift off MONTAUBAN at 2.25.
A/51.	MARLBORO WOOD.	
B/51.	Western corner of MONTAUBAN.	Orchards & houses just east of Right Group boundary.
C/51.	CATERPILLAR WOOD.	MARICOURT Section to enfilade western portion of wood.
D/51.	CATERPILLAR WOOD.	On Centre Group Front.

PHASE <u>VIII</u>. - 2.30 onwards.

Wire Cutting Batteries.	Barrage "H".	Steady rate of fire, periodic bursts of fire, and ready to turn on intense fire if necessary.
D/82, D/83, D/84.	CATERPILLAR WOOD on respective Group fronts.	During this phase forward observation must be obtained as soon as possible, and barrage regulated by actual observation and reports from Liason Officer.
A/51.	-do-	
B/51.	-do-	
C/51.	-do-	
D/51.	MARLBORO WOOD.	

C.A. Brooks
Captain, R.A.,
Brigade Major, R.A., 18th Division.

H.Q., R.A., 18/Div.
27th June, 1916.

Copies to all concerned.

APPENDIX "C".

APPROXIMATE allotment of ammunition for various tasks.

N.B. This table is worked out for one gun of a wire cutting battery.

DAY.	TASK.	18-prs:	4.5" How:	T.M. 2"	240 mm
"U" day & U/V Night	Wire cutting 18-prs: at rate of 200 rounds per gun.	200.			
	Approaches & Communications at night, about 2 Batts: per Group, to consist of about 12 salvoes per hour. N.B. Night from 8 PM to 5 AM.	100	60		
	18-prs. preventing repair of wire.	30.			
	TOTAL	320.	60.	–	–
"V" Day & V/W Night	Wire cutting.	200.		100.	
	O.Ps, Machine Gun emplacements, Communication trenches.		100.		
	Concentration of fire, Right Group.	10.	10.		
	Approaches & communications at night.	100.	50.		
	Gas barrage if required.	50.	30.		
	Preventing repair of wire and trenches.	20.			
	TOTAL	380.	190.	100.	–
"W" Day & W/X Night	Wire cutting.	200.		100.	
	O.Ps, Machine Guns, Communication trenches, etc.		100.		30.
	Concentration of fire, Left Group.	10.	10.		
	Approaches & Communications at night.	100.	50.		
	Preventing repair of wire & trenches.	30.	10.		
	Gas barrage if not fired on previous night.				
	TOTAL	340.	170.	100.	30.

(2) (Appendix "C" contd.)

DAY.	TASK.	18-prs:	4.5" How:	T.M. 2"	240 mm
"X" Day & X/Y Night	Wire cutting.	200.		40.	
	O.Ps, Machine guns, trenches, etc.		100.	40.	30.
	Concentration of fire one battery per group.	10.	10.		
	Approaches & Communications at night.	100.	50.		
	Preventing repair of wire and trenches.	30.	10.		
	Gas barrage if not fired on previous night.				
	TOTAL:	340.	170.	80.	30.
"Y" Day & Y/Z Night	Wire Cutting.	200.		30.	
	O.Ps, Machine Guns, trenches, etc.		100.	30.	30.
	Concentration of fire Centre Group.	10.	10.		
	Approaches & Communications at night.	100.	50.		
	Preventing repair of wire and trenches.	40.	20.	30.	
	TOTAL:	350.	180.	90.	30.
"Z" Day up to assault.	65 minute bombardment at about 3 rounds per gun per minute (18-pr.) N.B. 4.5" Ammunition possibly S.K. during this period.	200.	125.	30.	10.
	TOTAL:	200.	125.	30.	10.

(Appendix "C" contd.)

TOTALS per Gun previous to Assault.

	18-prs:	4.5" Howr:	T.M. 2".	240 mm.
"U" Day & U/V Night	320.	50.		
"V" " & V/W "	380.	190.	100.	
"W" " & W/X "	340.	170.	100.	30.
"X" " & X/Y "	340.	170.	80.	30.
"Y" " & Y/Z "	350.	180.	90.	30.
"Z" day up to assault	200.	125.	30.	10.
TOTAL:	1930.	885.	400.	100.

Rough estimate of expenditure from 0.00 to 2.30 and remainder of "Z" day and night.

	18-prs:	4.5" Howr:	T.M. 2".	240 mm.
During assault at rate of approximately 3 rounds per gun per minute 18-pr: and 2 rounds per gun in minute for 4.5" How:	500. *(300)*	250.		
For barrages, special undertakings, etc.	500.	250.		
TOTAL:	1000.	500.		
Total up to 0.00 time	2000.	1000.	430.	100.
GRAND TOTAL:	3000.	1500.	530.	100.

600

APPENDIX "D".

PREPARATIONS FOR FORWARD ADVANCE.

(1) **GENERAL PRINCIPLES GOVERNING DISPOSITIONS FOR FORWARD MOVE.**

The general principle on which the forward move of batteries will be carried out is briefly as under:-

   (a) The Three Group System, with each Group supporting its own Infantry Brigade, will be adhered to throughout.

   (b) Certain batteries from each Group have been placed in forward positions to form an advanced basis, to be reinforced by batteries of the same Group as occasion arises.

   (c) The 18-pr. batteries of the 50th Brigade, R.F.A., have been distributed amongst the three Groups in such a manner as to be available to move forward or be detached as a complete Brigade, at a short notice, without seriously affecting the efficiency of the Groups supporting the Infantry Brigades.

   (d) Certain single guns have been so placed as to be able to bring close range and enfilade fire in the initial stages, and to be available for a very early move forward in close support of the infantry.

(2) **DISPOSITIONS FOR FORWARD MOVE.**

The following batteries in each Group will hold themselves in readiness for a probable early move during the operations :-

   Left Group :- B/82 & A/85.
   Centre " :- A/83 & B/85.
   Right " :- B/84 & C/84.

The positions to be occupied by these batteries, and routes to them, are shown in attached diagram.

Group Commanders will ensure that bridges are prepared where necessary, the forward positions thoroughly reconnoitred, and every possible preliminary preparations made to enable these positions to be occupied without delay when required.

(3) **ORDER OF ADVANCE.**

The order of advance will necessarily depend on circumstances. In all probability one battery per group will first be moved forward.

(4) **SINGLE GUNS FOR CLOSE SUPPORT OF INFANTRY.**

The two single guns at F.17.b.2.2. and F.12.c.7.3. will hold themselves in readiness to be moved forward at an early hour during the proceedings.

It may not be possible to bring limbers and teams up in sufficient time to move these guns, every preparation should consequently be made to man handle these guns forward if necessary. Sufficient drag ropes, picks and shovels will be kept in these emplacements for this purpose. In

addition

(Appendix "D" cont'd.)

(2).

addition to the above 6 iron girders per gun will be held ready to form trough bridges for the wheels of guns to assist in crossing trenches.

Every possible use will be made of infantry trench bridges and floor boards in improvising bridges for guns during the advance.

Line of Advance "A" shown on attached diagram will probably afford the best route for a forward move leading to positions in the vicinity of POMMIERS TRENCH.

In the event of it being necessary to man handle guns forward, a fatigue party from W/18 will be provided to assist in moving the guns forward, and in the supply of ammunition.

(5) LINES OF ADVANCE BEYOND OUR FORWARD TRENCH.

The attached diagram indicates roughly the forward lines of advance which it is hoped to open up shortly after the assault.

(6) ADVANCED SITES FOR WAGON LINES.

Advanced sites for wagons lines of batteries detailed to hold themselves in readiness are being reconnoitred at present. They will probably be sited in GROVETOWN VALLEY or in BILLON WOOD Valley.

Reference

Artillery lifts shewn by coloured lines.

Times on the left shew Heavy Art. lifts.
   "   "   " Right " Div¹ " "

Strong Pts. •
Russian Saps. —
Commⁿ Trenches —
Trench Mortars •
Visual Signalling Station —

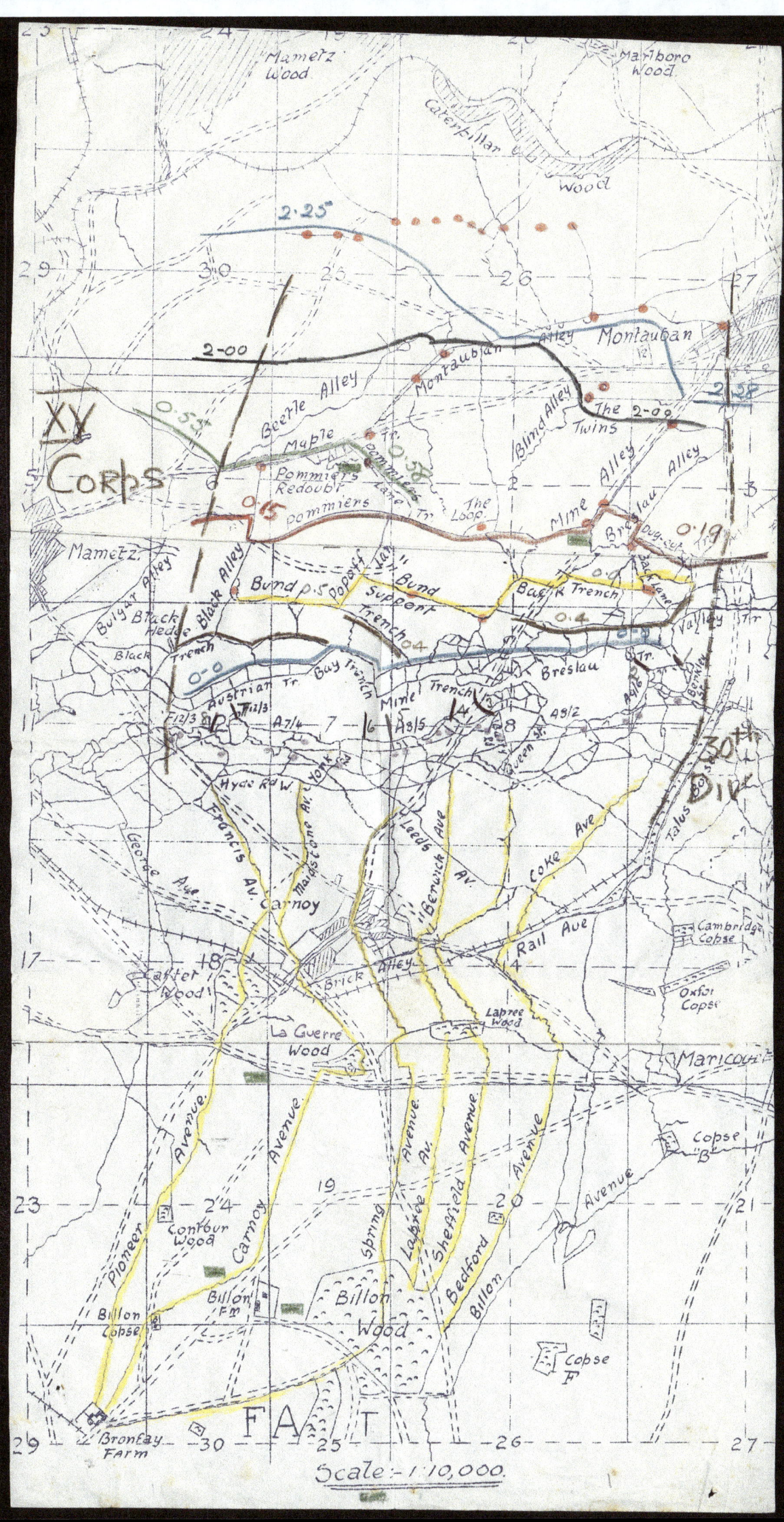

FORWARD ROUTES TO BE OPENED
UP BY R.E. AS SOON AS POSSIBLE.
— — — LEFT GROUP LINE OF ADVANCE
—··—··— CENTRE ,, ,, ,, ,,
—·—·— RIGHT ,, ,, ,, ,,

SECRET.

AMENDMENTS TO 18TH DIVISIONAL ARTILLERY ORDER NO. 1

(1) Owing to certain alterations in the Fourth Army "Programme for Preliminary Bombardment" the following amendments are forwarded.

(2) Appendix "A" "Programme for Preliminary Bombardment" issued with Operation Order No. 1 will be amended with the following instructions.

(3) Para. 14 should be added to follow para. 13 :-

(14) DISCHARGE OF SMOKE.

In order to lead the enemy to believe that an assault is about to be made, and induce him to man his front trenches, smoke will be discharged for the last 5 to 10 minutes of the times laid down for concentrated bombardments on "W", "X" and "Y" days.

The discharge of smoke will be accompanied by a heavy shrapnel barrage on front line and support trenches by all wire cutting batteries and searching of communication trenches by 4.5" howitzers for 5 minutes as under :-

    Front trench,   2 minutes.
    Lift to support line,   2   "
    Return to front line,   1 minute.

(4) "V" DAY.

XIII Corps H.A. will not require any time reserved for front trenches, the times allotted for this purpose are consequently re-allotted as under :-

    11 A.M. to 12.30 P.M. for 18 prs. wire cutting.
    3 P.M. to 5.00 P.M. " 2" T.H's wire cutting.

in addition to times already allotted.

The concentration of Right Group on MONTAUBAN between 4 P.M. and 4.20 P.M. is cancelled.

(5) "W" DAY.

18-pr. wire cutting batteries from 10.30 A.M. to 1 P.M. and 4 P.M. to 8 P.M. instead of 10 A.M. to 1 P.M., etc.

Add :-

10.15 A.M. to 10.20 A.M., 18-prs. intense bombardment of front and support trenches, and 4.5" howitzer batteries on communications in support of smoke discharge.

(6)   "X" DAY.

Cancel concentration detailed for 6 P.M. to 7 P.M. and substitute :-

4.30 A.M. to 5.30 A.M., 18-prs. and 4.5" howitzers concentration of Right Group wire cutting batteries on MONTAUBAN.

5.45 A.M. to 5.50 A.M., 18-prs. & 4.5" howitzers intense fire in support of smoke discharge, similar to "W" day.

(7)   "Y" DAY.

Times for concentration of Centre Group are altered to read from 6 A.M. to 7 A.M. instead of 6.0 to 7.20 A.M.

Add :-

7.15 A.M. to 7.20 A.M., 18-prs. & 4.5" howitzers, intense fire in support of smoke discharge similar to "W" day.

(8)   The above alterations will affect Appendix "C" slightly, Group Commanders should consequently consider these slight alterations :-

"V". Concentration of Right Group should now be considered under "X" day expenditure, whereas the expenditure allowed for concentration on "X" day may now be cancelled.

An additional expenditure of 15 rounds of 18-pr. and 10 rounds of 4.5" per gun should be added to "W", "X" and "Y" days for intense bombardment in support of discharge of gas.

(9)   The above amendments are so typed as to allow cutting out and adding to appendices in their respective places.

                                            CAPTAIN, R.A.
                            BRIGADE MAJOR, 18th DIV. ARTILLERY.

18TH DIVISIONAL ARTILLERY OPERATION ORDER NO. 3
- by -
Brigadier General S.F. Metcalfe, D.S.O.

July 6th. 1916.

---

(1) In continuation of 18th Divisional Artillery Operation Order No. 2 the XV Corps will attack MAMETZ WOOD at 8 A.M. on 7th inst.

(2) The Artillery of XIII Corps will cooperate as follows :-

Fire will commence at 7.20 A.M. and cease 10.30 A.M. with an intense period between 7.50 A.M. and 8.30 A.M.

(a) 18th Divisional Artillery.

  I. Bombard MARLBORO TRENCH from 250 yards North of MARLBORO WOOD to S.14.d.42.14.

  II. Bombard SABOT & FLATIRON COPSES.

  III. Bombard the german 2nd line from S.14.d.42.14 to S.W. corner of BAZENTIN LE PETIT WOOD.

  IV. Bombard the fence running from S.14.d.42.14 to FLAT IRON COPSE.

  N.B. Ammunition allowed 4000 rounds 18-pr. and 1000 rounds 4.5" How:

(b) Corps Heavy Artillery.

  Tasks as for 18th Divisional Artillery, 600 rounds of 6" How:

(3) F.O.Os are to look out for machine guns in above places and to endeavour to destroy them.

(4) After 10.30 A.M. the 18th Divisional Artillery will be ready to deal with a counter attack and will search woods and villages behind the german 2nd line occasionally.

(5) Tasks described in para. 2 are allotted to Groups as under :-

Left Group :-

German 2nd line from S.W.corner of BAZENTIN LE PETIT S.7.d.3.1. to S.14 central, with 4.5" how: battery on trench junctions at S.13.b.5.8. and S.13.b.8.8.

Centre Group:-

SABOT COPSE, FLATIRON COPSE and hedge between FLATIRON COPSE and S.14.d.42.14 with 4.5" how: battery on FLATIRON & SABOT COPSES.

Right Group:-

Enfilade MARLBORO TRENCH and German 2nd line from 250 yards North of MARLBORO COPSE to S.14 central, with 4.5" how: battery searching above trench.

(6). Ammunition.

-2-

(6) <u>Ammunition</u> :-

1300 rounds 18-pr. and 330 rounds of 4.5" how: ammunition per Group - Rate of fire, moderate, with intense period from 7.50 A.M. to 8.30 A.M.

(7) Groups will endeavour to carry out all possible registration necessary from dawn to the hour of attack.

(8) All F.O.Os. will forward frequent reports as to progress of operation, and movements of the enemy - They will be ready to engage any hostile troops moving between MAMETZ WOOD and 2nd line, and keep a special look out for hostile machine guns.

(9) Tasks laid down in para. 4 will be carried out as under :-

From 10.30 A.M. Left & Centre Groups will keep sharp look out for counter attacks between MAMETZ WOOD & BAZENTIN WOODS - Right Group will search both BAZENTIN WOODS and roads between these woods.

(10) 49th Siege of 6" How: will be held in readiness to deal with any contingency that may occur, and should keep the whole ground in question under close observation.

(11) PLEASE ACKNOWLEDGE BY WIRE.

Captain, R.A.,
Brigade Major, R.A., 18th Division.

H.Q., R.A., 18/Div.

Copies to:-

Right Group.
Centre Group.
Left Group.
49th Siege Battery.
18th Division.
38th Division.
XIII Corps R.A.

War Diary

18th Div. Art. Operation Order No. 2.

July 6th 1916.

1. XV Corps are carrying out a preliminary attack against the trenches to the S.W. of MAMETZ WOOD at 2 a.m. on 7th inst.

2. The Artillery of the 18th Division will cooperate as follows:-

Fire to commence at 1.40 a.m. and cease at 2.30 a.m.

(a) <u>18-pdrs.</u>

Barrage Eastern and Northern Edges of MAMETZ WOOD from S.19.d.80.85 to X.18.a.20.40
Ammunition allowed 2000 rounds.

(b) <u>4.5" Howitzers.</u>

Shell cross roads in Middle of MAMETZ WOOD at X.24.a.85.95
Ammunition allowed 100 rounds.

3. The above bombardment will be carried out by Left and Centre Groups as under.

Left Group. X.18.a.20.40 to S.13.d.8.9.

Centre Group. S.13.d.8.9. to S.19.d.80.85.

One 4.5" Howitzer of each Group on Cross Roads *tracks* at X.24.a.85.95.

4. Centre Group will ensure the fire on edge of MAMETZ WOOD at S.19.d.9.9. not endangering our outposts in North Western corner of CATERPILLAR WOOD.

5. 1000 rds. 18-pr. and 50 rds 4.5" Hows. ammunition allotted to ~~Right~~ *Centre* and Left Groups respectively.

6. The above bombardment should not interfere with bombardment of 2nd Line more than is absolutely necessary.

7. Please Acknowledge.

Captain R.A.,
Brigade Major R.A., 18th Division.

6/7/16.

Copies to:-
    Right)
    Centre) Groups.
    Left)
    18th Division.
    38th Division.

SECRET.
3rd Div.Arty.O.O.No.3   13/7/16.   COPY NO. 5

1. The 3rd Div.will attack the enemy 2nd line from S.16.b.6.2 to point S.15.c.15.40 on 14th instant.

2. The tasks of the 3rd Div.Arty.and 18th Div.Arty.on this front are attached in accompanying table.
   Till the attack, wire cutting and bombardments continue as at present.

3. During the attack, if 3rd Div.Arty.Bde.H.Q.are not close to Infantry Bde.H.Q., there must be an Artillery Liaison Officer with the latter.
   Telephone lines for F.O.O's are to be run as far forward as possible by 3rd D.A.batteries during the 12th and 13th with the object of having one F.O.O.with each battn.on capture of the objective.
   B.C's and F.O.O's to have a copy of tasks, objectives and times of "lifts" with them, and also 1/20,000 MARTINPUICH map.

4. When the objective is gained, the Div.Arty.take over the defence of the line and must have their Brigade H.Q.near Inf.bde.H.Q. and F.O.O's with Battn.Commanders.

5. The 84th Bde.R.F.A. 18th Div.will move under orders of C.R.A. 3rd Division to positions they have reconnoitred. Two batteries of this Brigade will be in readiness to move at short notice. One wagon per gun will accompany these Batteries.

6. Watches will be synchronised twice over the telephone - 6 p.m. and 12 midnight preceding Zero hour.

7. 3rd D.A.18-pr batteries should have 700 rounds at each gun on the morning of the attack; howitzers 400 rounds per gun.
   18th D.A.18-pr batteries should have 500 and 300 rounds respectively.
   After the attack batteries of both Divisions should keep up to 500 18-pr and 300 How.

8. O.C.40th Brigade will detail one Battery to be ready to advance with the 76th Infantry brigade. The roads forward should be reconnoitred and arrangements made with the R.E.for crossing trenches.
   As soon as this Battery is ordered forward an officer will report to O.C.76th Bde.
   The 40th Brigade will work during the Time Table under orders of C.R.A.9th Division, until 1 hr. 30 min. after zero, when the Brigade will come under orders of C.R.A.3rd Division.
   The C.R.A.9th Division will arrange telephone communication through D/50 battery to 50th R.F.A.Bde.H.Q.which are with 27th Inf. Bde.
   40th Bde.Need not detail a Liaison Officer for 27th Inf.Bde.in MONTAUBAN.

9. In the case of batteries moving forward, dumps left behind in the old positions must be taken forward and used up before drawing from any other source.

10. C.R.A's Headquarters will be at F.30.c., 200 yards East of BRONFAY FARM from 3 p.m.13th instant, onwards.

P.T.O.

11. ACKNOWLEDGE.

D. N. Graham
Major R.A.
Brigade Major, 3rd Div. Arty.

Issued at 9 a.m.

No.1	23rd Bde.R.F.A.	8	3rd Div. 'G'
" 2	40th "	9	War Diary
" 3	42nd "	10	File
" 4	82nd "	11	R.A. XIII Corps.
" 5	83rd "	12	R.A. 18th Div.
" 6	84th "	13	76th Inf. bde.
" 7	R.A. 9th Div.		

EXPLANATION OF ATTACHED TIME TABLE.

The 3rd Division's front has been shortened. They will now attack on the front from S.15.c.1.4 to S.16.b.5.1, both points inclusive.
The 9th Division attack from S.16.b.5.1 eastwards.
The Infantry will be within 300 yards of front line before assaulting.
The Artillery commence shooting 5 minutes before the Infantry assault.
The Infantry assault at "Zero hour" and capture enemy's first line.
At 0 hours 5 minutes the Infantry assault and capture the support line from S.15 central to S.16.b.6.4 - but the left flank remains in the front line, necessitating one battery keeping a barrage on S.E. corner of BAZENTIN.
The object of the Howrs. from 0 hrs. 5 mins. to 1 hr. 35 mins. is to destroy BAZENTIN LE GRAND.
At 1 hours the Infantry capture the West End of support line from S. end of BAZENTIN to BAZENTIN WOOD.
At 1.35 hours the Infantry begin to advance through village and to the line of road and hedge from X roads S.17.b.½.9½ to S.16.b.0.8.
The barrage from S.9.c.4.4 to S.10.d.5.4 will be known as "North Barrage".
The 40th Brigade R.F.A. are attached to the 9th Division till 1 hour 30 minutes after Zero; they then come under orders of C.R.A. 3rd Division and will stand by to help thicken the North Barrage from S.9.c.4.4 to S.10.d.5.4

* * *

General Scheme to accompany Time Table.

-5 to Zero	) 18-prs on enemy's wire) 4.5's on selected points.
Zero to 0.5'	) 18 prs & 4.5's on Support line.
0.5' to 1 hr. 35'	) All 18 prs. 200 yards North of Support line) (except one battery of 18th Div. Left Group)) All 4.5's concentrated on BAZENTIN
1 hr 35' to 1 hr 40'	) All guns increase their range about 100 yards.
1 hr 40' onwards.	) All guns and hows lift to a line 200 yards North) of the line along S. edge of squares S.9,10.

SECRET

TIME TABLE.

		Left Groups	Centre Group	Right Group of 18th Division only	Rates of fire 18pr. Hows: ½ as fast.
-5'	18-pr	Enemy's wire	Enemy's wire	Enemy's support line	(4 rounds per gun per min for first
	Hows.	S.15.c.0.4 to S.15.d.0.8 Selected points in front & support trenches as in b.M.22 of 11/7/16.	S.15.d.0.8 to S.16 central Selected points in front & support trenches as in b.M.22 of 11/7/16.	S.15.a.2.1 to S.15.b.5.6	3 min. 6 rounds per gun per min.last 2 minutes.
Zero hour	18 pr Hows	Support trench S.15.a.2.1 to S.15.b.0.1	Support trench S.15.b.0.1 to S.16.b.0.5	ditto ditto	
0.5'	18 pr Hows	S.15.a.3.4 to S.15.b.3.4 S.15.a.9.3 to S.15.b.3.3	S.15.b.3.4 to S.10.d.0.0 S.15.a.9.3 to S.15.b.3.3	S.15.a.3.4 to S.10.d.0.0 S.15.a.9.3 to S.15.b.3.3	(3 rounds per gun per min. to 0 hr. 20 mins. After-
(1 hr '30')	18 pr Hows	S.15.a.3.3 to S.15.b.8.9 S.15.a.9.6 to S.15.b.5.6	S.15.b.0.9 to S.10.d.3.1 S.15.a.9.6 to S.15.b.5.6	S.15.a.3.6 to S.10.d.3.1 S.15.a.9.6 to S.15.b.5.6	wards 1 round per gun per minute. Guns & Hows.firing
(1 hr 40' onwards	18 pr Hows	S.9.c.4.4 to S.9.d.8.4 - ditto -	S.9.d.8.4 to S.10.d.5.4 - ditto -	S.9.c.4.4 to S.10.d.5.4	on BAZENTIN will fire 2 rds.& 1 rd respectively per min.from 0 hr 5' to 1 hr 35 min.

± 50%

Batteries will fire shrapnel from -5 mins to 0 hrs.5 mins., after 0.hr 5 mins 25% H.E.will be used.

Orders for 40th Bde.R.F.A.from -5 to 1 hr.30' will be issued by C.R.A.9th Div.

Above cancels Table b.M.13

13/7/16

W.M.Graham
Major R.A.
Bde.Major, 3rd Div.Arty.

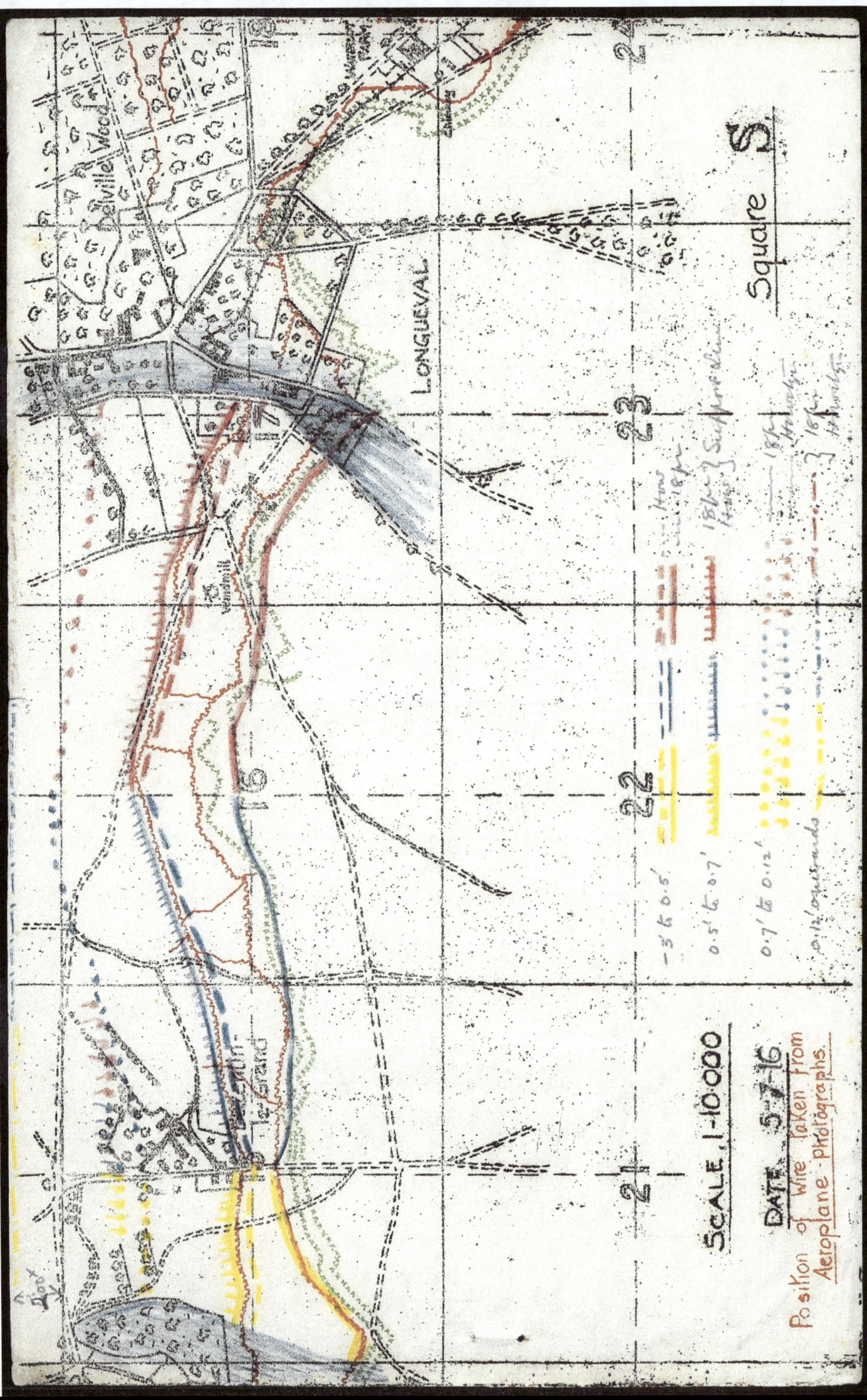

"JANE"

UNIT.	SERIAL NUMBER.	DESCRIPTION.
DIVISIONAL UNIT.	1802	Divisional H.Q.
82nd BRIGADE R.F.A.	1840	Brigade H.Q.
	1841	'A' Batty. R.F.A. 4 - 18 Pdrs.
	1842	'B' " " 4 - 18 "
	1843	'C' " " 4 - 18 "
	1844	'D' " " 4 Howitzers.
83rd BRIGADE R.F.A.	1850	Brigade H.Q.
	1851	'A' Batty. R.F.A. 4 - 18 Pdrs.
	1852	'B' " " 4 - 18 "
	1853	'C' " " 4 - 18 "
	1854	'D' " " 4 Howitzers.
84th BRIGADE R.F.A.	1860	Brigade H.Q.
	1861	'A' Batty. R.F.A. 4 - 18 Pdrs
	1862	'B' " " 4 - 18 "
	1863	'C' " " 4 - 18 "
	1864	'D' " " 4 Howitzers.
85th BRIGADE R.F.A.	1870	Brigade H.Q.
	1871	'A' Batty. R.F.A. 4 - 18 Pdrs.
	1872	'B' " " 4 - 18 "
	1873	'C' " " 4 - 18 "
DIVISIONAL AMMUNITION COLUMN.	1878	H.Q. Div.Amm.Column.
	1879	No.1 Sec.Div.Amm.Col.)
	1880	No.2 " " " ") Echelon 'A'
	1881	No.3 " " " ")
	1882	No.4 " " " " Echelon 'B'
	1896	'Y' 18. T.Mortar Battery.
	1897	'X' 18. T.Mortar Battery.
	1898	'Z' 18. T.Mortar Battery.
	1899A	'V' 18. T.Mortar Battery.
	1899B	'W' 18. T.Mortar Battery.

To each Battery 1 G.S. Supply and 1 G.S. Baggage Wagon.

F.I. Leslie Ditmas.
Captain for Major.
A.D.R.T.(IV)

AMIENS.
July 24th 1916.

MOVE OF 18th DIVISION (ARTILLERY)

from FOURTH ARMY   to SECOND ARMY.

A   PONT REMY   Regulating Station

B   LONGPRE   ST. OMER.

	Train No. from Stations		Serial No.	Date	Marche	Time of departure	Time due to arrive	Remarks
	A.	B.						
1	2	3	4	5	6	7	8	9
	1	-	1850, 51, 80	26/7/16	T15	20.48		
	-	2	1840, 41, 79	"	16	22.31		
	3	-	1852, 80	"	18	23.58		
	-	4	1842, 79	27/7/16	19	1.01		
	5	-	1853, 80	"	21	2.58		
	-	6	1843, 79	"	22	3.11		
	7	-	1854, 80	"	24	5.58		
	-	8	1844, 79	"	1	6.41		
	9	-	1860, 61, 81	"	3	8.58		
	-	10	1870, 71, 97	"	4	9.41		
	11	-	1862, 81	"	6	12.08		
	-	12	1872, 96, 02	"	7	12.21		
	13	-	1863, 81	"	9	14.41		
	-	14	1873, 78, 98	"	10	15.58		
	15	-	1864, 81	"	12	17.58		
	-	16	1882($\frac{1}{2}$), 99A	"	13	18.41		T.P.
	17	-	1882($\frac{1}{2}$), 99B	"	15	20.48		T.P.

SUMMARY

PONT REMY   (A)   8 t.cs.   1 t.p.
LONGPRE   (B)   7 t.cs.   1 t.p.

AMIENS.
24th July 1916.

F. Leslie Ditmas.
Captain
for Major,
A.D.R.T.(IV)

TIME TABLE.

LONGPRE STATION.

22-31   A/82 Battery (and 2 G.S.Wagons 5 Amm.Wagons from D.A.C.)
1-01   B/82   "   "   "   "   "   "   "   "   "   "
3-11   C/82   "   "   "   "   "   "   "   "   "   "
6-41   D/82   "   "   "   "   "   "   "   "   "   "
        N.B. 82nd Bde. Hd. Qrs. distributed in above trains.

9-41   A/85 (and 2 G.S.wagons from D.A.C.) H.Q.18th Div.Art.,
                                            X/18 T. M. B.
12-21   B/85 ("   "   "   "   "   ) H.Q. 85th Bde. R.F.A.
                                            Y/18 T. M. B.
15-58. C/85 ("   "   "   "   "   ) Z/18 T. M. B.
        N.B. 150th Co. A.S.C. (28 pairs of wheels) will be distributed
             amongst trains of 85th Brigade, R.F.A.

18-41   ½ No.4 Section D.A.C.(less G.S.wagons provided for batteries)
        about 42 pairs of wheels.
        Hd.Qrs.,D.A.C.
        2 Ambulance Wagons.
        V/18 Trench Mortar Battery.

PONT REMY STATION.

20-48   A/83 Battery (& 2 G.S.wagons 5 Amm.Wagons from D.A.C.)
23-58   B/83   "   "   "   "   "   "   "   "   "   "
2-58   C/83   "   "   "   "   "   "   "   "   "   "
5-58   D/83   "   "   "   "   "   "   "   "   "   "
        N.B. 83rd Bde. H.Q. distributed in above trains.

8-58   A/84 Battery (& 2 G.S.Wagons 5 Amm.Wagons from D.A.C.)
12-08   B/84   "   "   "   "   "   "   "   "   "   "
14-41   C/84   "   "   "   "   "   "   "   "   "   "
17-58   D/84   "   "   "   "   "   "   "   "   "   "
        N.B. 84th Bde. H.Q. distributed in above trains.

20-48   ½ No. 4 Section D.A.C. about 42 pairs of wheels.
        15 limbered G.S.wagons from Nos. 1, 2 & 3 Sections D.A.C.
        W/18 T. M. B.

SECRET.

A.B.No.240/72.

18TH DIVISIONAL ARTILLERY ORDER NO. 5
- by -
BRIGADIER GENERAL S.F. METCALFE, D.S.O.

(1) The 18th Divisional Artillery will entrain at LONGPRE and PONT REMY on the 26th and 27th, and will move by rail from Fourth Army to V Corps Second Army as shown in attached table.

(2) Trains are allotted at the rate of one train per battery, and 2 trains for No. 4 Section of Div. Amm. Col. The remaining units will be distributed amongst trains as under.

(3) The Div. Amm. Col. will provide 2 G.S. wagons for each battery and Brigade Headquarters, namely 38 G.S. wagons. These wagons include those already with 82, 83 & 85th Brigades, R.F.A.

In addition to the above 5 ammunition wagons will be entrained with each battery of the 82nd, 83rd & 84th Brigades namely 30 ammunition wagons in all (48 18-pr & 12 4.5" howitzer wagons)

The above wagons & G.S. wagons will remain with the batteries they entrain with, and will be rationed by them, until receipt of further orders.

(4) No. 4 Section of the Div. Amm. Column and any vehicles not entrained with batteries will entrain in Nos. 16 & 17 trains.

In addition 2 Ambulance wagons, and two heavy trench mortar batteries will entrain in these trains as shown in attached table.

(5) The three Medium Trench Mortar Batteries will entrain with batteries of 85th Brigade, R.F.A. The 84th Brigade will provide necessary G.S. wagons to convey Medium Mortars and baggage of V/18 battery from ERONDELLE to LONGPRE on the afternoon of the 26th, on application from 18th Divisional Trench Mortar Officer.

(6) Wagons as detailed in para. 3 will be transferred from Div. Amm. Col. to Brigades on the afternoon of 26th as under:-

10 G.S. wagons and teams to 84th Brigade.
20 Ammunition wagons and teams to 82nd Brigade.
20   "   "   "   "   " 83rd   "
20   "   "   "   "   " 84th   "

(7) All units will arrive at the station three hours before the advertised time of departure, but will not enter the station yard until the previous unit has finished entraining.

(8) Brigade Headquarters will be distributed amongst the trains of their respective Brigades. A representative from each Brigade Headquarters will remain behind so as to travel in the last train of the Brigade.

(9) Entraining facilities at both stations are poor. Brigade and Battery representatives should visit their respective stations previous to entraining to decide on best method.

Only one moveable ramp is at present available at LONGPRE for entraining horses.

(10) A working

(10)   A working party of 100 men will report to R.T.O's
PONT REMY and LONGPRE at 9 P.M. and 10.30 P.M. respectively.
These parties will be found as under :-

   PONT REMY   - 9 P.M.,   W/18 & 40 men from 84th Bde.
   LONGPRE   -10.30 P.M., V/18 & 30 men each from 82nd &
                                            85th Brigades.

(11)   Trains 1 to 15 are T.C. trains consisting of 14 flats,
34 covers and 1 coach for officers.
   Trains 16 & 17 are T.F. trains consisting of 23 flats,
24 covers and 1 coach for officers.

(12)   The 150th Company, A.S.C. (28 pairs of wheels) will entrain
with 85th Brigade, 1/3rd of the Company in each train.

(13)   The journey will probably be about a 10 hours run -
Detraining stations ARQUES & WIZERNES.

(14)   Orders as to billets in new area will be issued on
arrival at detraining stations.

(15)   Rations for consumption on the 26th will be drawn on the
morning of 25th at 9 A.M. and will be carried in the supply
wagons.

                                                   Capt. T Brook
                                            Captain, R.A.,
                                   Brigade Major, R.A., 18th Division.

H.Q., R.A., 18/Div.
25th July, 1916.

Copies to :-

   Headquarters, 18/Div. ('G' & 'Q'.) (2)
   18th Divisional Train.   (1)
   82nd Brigade, R.F.A.   (5)
   83rd   "   "   (5)
   84th   "   "   (5)
   85th   "   "   (4)
   Divnl. Amm. Column.   (5)
   Div. Trench Mortar Officer.   (1)
   V/18 H. T. M. B.,   (1)
   W/18 " " " "   (1)
   R. T. O. LONGPRE.   (1)
   R. T. O. PONT REMY.   (1)
   150th Company, A.S.C.   (1)
   Supply Officer Div. Troops.   (1)
   Detached Section Div. Supply Column.(1)

WAR DIARY
or
INTELLIGENCE SUMMARY
(Erase heading not required.)

Army Form C. 2118

83rd Brigade R.F.A. Vol XIII

Place	Date	Hour	Summary of Events and Information	Remarks and references to Appendices
CAESTRE	1.8.16		Bde Hd Qrs at CAESTRE, all batteries in camp in neighbourhood of EECKE. Guns are being overhauled by I.O.M. and batteries refitting.	
	2.8.16		Nothing to report	
	3.8.16		Brigade marched to ERQUINGHEM via BAILLEUL, STEENWERCK and CROIX du BAC. Bde Hd Qrs went into billet at RUE MARLE. ARMENTIERS.	
		11 p.m.	"C" and "D" Batteries occupied position. Bde Sagnam rejoined	
ARMENTIERS	4.8.16		Brigade in relieving right group NEW ZEALAND Artillery. "C" and "D" Batteries registered points in new zone	
	5.8.16	9 p.m.	"A" and "B" Batteries occupied positions. All Batteries registered points in new zone, completed telephone communications with O.Ps and Btn H.Q. Positions are A/83 1 Sec I 7 d 2.3. 1 Sec I 7 d 9.5. B/83 I 1 D 5. 3. C/83 I 8 a 7. 2. D/83 I 8 a 5. 5. Brigade covers left batalion front of 18 Div and west 82nd Bde, which covers right batalion of left brigade, form left group R.A. 18 Div under orders of Lt Col Sagnam. 5th Inf Bde held the front covered by this group, two batallions in the line and one in reserve.	Reference BOIS GRENIER Sheet 36 N.W. 4
	6.8.16		Nothing to return	
	7.8.16		" " "	
	8.8.16		" " "	

Army Form C. 2118.

WAR DIARY
or
INTELLIGENCE SUMMARY.

(Erase heading not required.)

83rd Bde. R.F.A.

Instructions regarding War Diaries and Intelligence Summaries are contained in F.S. Regs., Part II. and the Staff Manual respectively. Title pages will be prepared in manuscript.

Place	Hour, Date	Summary of Events and Information	Remarks and references to Appendices
ARMENTIERS	9-8-16	Nothing to report	
	10.8.16	" "	
	11.8.16	" "	
	12.8.16	" "	
	13.8.16	Enemy artillery shelled ARMENTIERS.	
	14.8.16	Nothing to report	
	15.8.16	" "	
	16.8.16	" "	
	17.8.16	" "	
	18.8.16	Our batteries fired a scheme of aggression. Enemy did not retaliate	
	19.8.16	Our batteries fired scheme of aggression. Enemy retaliated with trench mortars. 4.5" How D/83 retaliated for enemy trench mortars. Orders received that 18 Div R.A. would be relieved by 3rd Div R.A.	
	20.8.16	10.45 a.m. Batteries fired at searchlight. Signal was given by Liason Officer. Searchlight disappeared. Nothing to report	
	21.8.16	Advance parties of 3rd Div Arty (160 Bde) arrived and were taken round positions and O.Ps.	
	22.8.16		
	23.8.16		
	24.8.16	9.30 a.m. Our section hr battery relieved by section of 160 Bde R.F.A. at Relieved section marched to wagon lines. Enemy shelled our trenches during the day. Our batteries fired a scheme of aggression at 7.15 a.m.	

Army Form C. 2118.

WAR DIARY
or
INTELLIGENCE SUMMARY.
(Erase heading not required.)

83rd Bde R.F.A.

Hour, Date, Place		Summary of Events and Information	Remarks and references to Appendices
ARMENTIERS	25. 8. 16	Relieved section of batteries and all wagons marched at 9 a.m. to concentration area near CROIX du BAC. Enemy shelled E. portion of ARMENTIERS.	
—	26. 8. 16	Remaining section of batteries relieved by 160 Bde R.F.A. Returns 9 and 9.30 a.m. Section marched to concentration area near CROIX du BAC. Bde Hd Qrs and personnel of Hd Qrs. 11 a.m. after which they marched to CROIX du BAC.	
CROIX du BAC	26. 8. 16	Batteries and Bde Hd Qrs in bivouac	
—	27. 8. 16	do	
—	28. 8. 16	Orders received that Brigade would entrain to 3rd ARMY area in vicinity of St POL. Later, orders to cancel that Brigade would proceed to vicinity of DOULLENS.	
—	29. 8. 16	Batteries entrained at BAILLEUL. Bde Hd Qrs entrained at BAILLEUL. Batteries & Bde Hd Qrs arrived at DOULLENS and marched to HEM.	
—	30. 8. 16	Brigade marched to vicinity of ALBERT	
—	31. 8. 16	Brigade came under orders of 2nd Australian Div Art at 9 a.m. O.C. and Bty commanders reconnoitred positions	

Chas G. Rifle
Col. 83rd Bde R.F.A.

Vol 124

83rd Bde R.F.A. — Army Form C. 2118.

WAR DIARY
or
INTELLIGENCE SUMMARY.
(Erase heading not required.)

Hour, Date, Place	Summary of Events and Information	Remarks and references to Appendices
ALBERT 1-9-16 5 a.m.	Batteries marched to take up positions S.W. of CONTALMAISON	
12 noon	Batteries in position and communication established	
Near CONTALMAISON 2-9-16	During the afternoon batteries registered points in zones. Enemy artillery fairly active. Battery positions are "A" X 21 a 4-4., "B" X 21 a 5-5. "C" X 15 d 9-1., "D" X 16 A Y-1 Bn HQ Bn X 16 C 1-1	
— 3-9-16 5.10 a.m.	Batteries registered by aid of aeroplane. Enemy artillery active along whole front. Australian infantry attacked MOUQUET FARM and enemy trenches to the east. All objective gained. Order received that 18 Div. Arty. would take over line at 5 p.m. New zones allotted and batteries registered.	
— 4-9-16	Batteries completed registration. Enemy artillery active all day and night	
— 5-9-16	During the day & night batteries fired bursts of enemy from line and approaches	
— 6-9-16	Nothing to report	
— 7-9-16	Enemy artillery and aircraft active all day. During the night enemy bombarded our trenches heavily. Our guns replied on his trenches and approaches	

WAR DIARY or INTELLIGENCE SUMMARY.

(Erase heading not required.)

83rd Bde R.F.A. Army Form C. 2118.

Hour, Date, Place	Summary of Events and Information	Remarks and references to Appendices
Near CONTALMAISON 8.9.16	Orders received that 2nd Can Bn would attack enemy trenches on 9th. Batteries fired bursts at trenches during the day and night. Enemy artillery active on POZIERS and CONTALMAISON	
9.9.16 4.45 p.m.	Attack carried out and objective gained. Our batteries barraged enemy front line for 3 minutes then lifted 200 yds and remained on that barrage for 20 minutes. About 60 prisoners and 2 machine guns captured. Enemy counter attacked during the night but were driven off. Captured trenches consolidated.	
10.9.16	Enemy artillery heavily bombarded Inf Bde & Bde Hd Qrs. Our batteries registered new line and fired bursts of fire during the day and night. Enemy artillery very active.	
11.9.16	"A" and "B" Batteries reconnoitered new positions in view of certain forthcoming operations. Positions selected at "A" x.16.a.4.6. "B" x.16.a.5.5. and work begun on them. Preliminary orders for attack received. Batteries registered. Enemy artillery active	
12.9.16	Work on new positions continued. Nothing to report	
13.9.16	Enemy artillery active. Work on new positions completed	
14.9.16	Orders received that the Canadian Corps would attack German positions between COURCELETTE and MARTIN PUICH. 83rd Bde are supporting 2nd Can Div. 3rd Canadian Div will attack on its Left and 15th Div on the right, in conjunction with 4th and Franch Armies.	

WAR DIARY
or
INTELLIGENCE SUMMARY.

(Erase heading not required.)

83rd Bde R.F.A. Army Form C. 2118.

Hour, Date, Place	Summary of Events and Information	Remarks and references to Appendices
NEAR CONTALMAISON 6·20 a.m. 15·9·16	Attack commenced. Artillery bombarded German front line from 0.F. 0.4 and then by lifts of 100 yds lifts then barrage to first objective, (namely running through M.30.b, R.32.c, R.36.a and M.31.b. This barrage was bombarded for 6 minutes and then fire lifted to a line 300 yds beyond. The Infantry attack was carried out according to programme, the enemy resistance was weak. "Tanks" were used for clearing trenches.	
7·33 a.m.	Barrage lifted to a line 300 yds east of road joining COURCELETTE and MARTINPUICH	
7·53 a.m.	Barrage dropped back to 300 yds beyond objective.	
6·15 p.m.	Canadian Corps attacked COURCELETTE. Artillery supported the attack by barrages lifting 100 yds under N and E of village was reached. Attack was successful and ground was consolidated.	
16·9·16	Enemy counter-attacked during the night, but was driven off	
	Zones on E and S.E of COURCELETTE allotted to batteries, registration carried out and barrages fired during Counter attack.	
17·9·16	C/83 moved to forward position 1000 yds S.E of POZIERS. All batteries completed registration and fired during night on new Zones.	
18·9·16	A, B and D moved to forward positions S.E of POZIERS	

WAR DIARY or INTELLIGENCE SUMMARY

Army Form C. 2118.

83rd Brigade R.F.A.

Hour, Date, Place	Summary of Events and Information	Remarks and references to Appendices
Noon CONTALMAISON 19-9-16	Batteries completed new positions and registered. Situation quiet during the day, but at night enemy made two attacks on our trenches E of COURCELETTE which were driven off.	
20. 9. 16	Nothing to report	
21. 9. 16	Enemy made small local attack of combined Infantry & Bombers. Fire on barrage line and dispersed enemy. Enemy artillery active.	
22. 9. 16	Nothing to report	
23. 9. 16	Canadian Infantry attacked powerhouse E of COURCELETTE at 8-30 p.m. Attack was successful. Enemy in was on wire and counter attack. Ground consolidated.	
24. 9. 16	Enemy shelled COURCELETTE at intervals during the day and night.	
25. 9. 16	Nothing to report	
26. 9. 16 12.35 p.m.	Canadian Corps attacked ridge running N.W. of COURCELETTE to SCHWABEN REDOUBT. 28th Batt. and barrage area E of COURCELETTE 83rd Bde. Artillery. 83rd, 84th and 83rd Bde. barraged area NE and N of COURCELETTE. The attack was carried out according to programme and objectives gained. Fire during the attack 83rd Bde engaged enemy batteries located by aircraft.	
6-30 p.m.	Liason Officer reported enemy holding trench E of COURCELETTE in force. Batteries engaged target causing enemy to retire across open followed by our barrage. Batteries noticed Nagg by aircraft of So Gaults Catch enemy in shell holes, and to a great extent were reached	

Forms/C. 2118/10.

WAR DIARY
or
INTELLIGENCE SUMMARY.

83rd Bde R.F.A.

Army Form C. 2118.

(Erase heading not required.)

Hour, Date, Place	Summary of Events and Information	Remarks and references to Appendices
Near CONTALMAISON 26.9.16	From 9pm to 9.30pm our batteries bombarded TVS. Gas approaches and DESTREMONT FARM were subjected to bursts of fire during the night.	
27.9.16	During the day enemy heavily shelled COURCELETTE. Nothing to report	
28.9.16	Enemy attacked ground games N.W. of COURCELETTE but were driven off. Battery shelled TVS. Enemy shelled new front line.	
29.9.16	Orders received that Bde moved to join 2nd Corps and come under orders of 18 Div. O.C. Bde and B.C. reconnoitred position	
30.9.16	Position selected S.W. of THIEPVAL occupied by batteries. Bde the gun just E of AVELUY. Batteries registered new 3ones	

[signature]
For Lieut Col RFA
Comdy 83rd /Bde RFA

War Diary
for
October 1916

83rd Bde.
R.F.A.

Army Form C. 2118.

9/909

83rd Bde R.F.a

WAR DIARY
or
INTELLIGENCE SUMMARY.
(Erase heading not required.)

Instructions regarding War Diaries and Intelligence Summaries are contained in F.S. Regs., Part II. and the Staff Manual respectively. Title pages will be prepared in manuscript.

Hour, Date, Place	Summary of Events and Information	Remarks and references to Appendices
1-10-16 near AVELUY	Batteries are in action in R.3.c. Bde H.Q. in R.1.8.c. Batteries are covering 18 Div Infantry. 83rd Bde. work has been laid out on STUFF TRENCH. Batteries registered, and work at new emplacements commenced	
2-10-16	Registration continued. Also work on new emplacements. Enemy artillery active on THIEPVAL	
3-10-16	Nothing to report	
4-10-16 7 a.m.	Enemy attacked with bombing parties on SCHWABEN REDOUBT 83rd Bde barrage front and enemy bombing parties were driven out.	
5. 10.10.16	Our front line and THIEPVAL heavily shelled during the day. Our batteries fired in retaliation and on communication and approaches	
6. 10.10.16	Nothing to report	
7. 10.10.16	Bde Commander and new Bde H.Q. at R.12.A.6.6. in AUTHUILLE WOOD.	
8. 10.10.16	Bde H.Q. moved into new position. Situation quiet	
9. 10.10.16 4.30 a.m.	117th Inf. Bde attacked the portion of SCHWABEN REDOUBT held by the enemy. Our Batteries barrages all roads and approaches to redoubt. The objective on right was gained but in centre and left no progress was made. Later our right was withdrawn to old line. Enemy attack heavily. Enemy attack	

WAR DIARY
or
INTELLIGENCE SUMMARY.

(Erase heading not required.)

83rd Bde R.F.A Army Form C. 2118.

Hour, Date, Place	Summary of Events and Information	Remarks and references to Appendices
AUTHUILLE WOOD		
12.35 p.m. 9.10.16	Our batteries co-operated with 25 Div in an attack on the portion of STUFF REDOUBT also held by the enemy. All objectives were gained and ground consolidated. Enemy artillery active during attack. Enemy counter attacked later, unsuccessfully.	
10.10.16	Nothing to report	
11.10.16	D/83 attached to II Corps for counter battery work. Enemy artillery bombarded our front line and THIEPVAL, our 18/r Batteries attacked.	
12.10.16	Batteries registered points on northern face of SCHWABEN REDOUBT prior to an attack by our infantry. Registration successful. Enemy left their trenches and surrendered.	
13.10.16	Nothing to report	
2.46 p.m. 14.10.16	118th Inf Bde attacked portion of SCHWABEN REDOUBT still held by the enemy. Two lines found the attacking party covered by 18th and 49th Div ART. The attack was carried out successfully. Programme and all objectives found, and ground consolidated. During the attack the enemy artillery was very active, but their barrage was 5 minutes late. No counter attack.	
8.30 p.m. 15.10.16	Enemy bombarded our new line N of SCHWABEN REDOUBT	
9 p.m.	S.O.S signal sent up. Enemy counter attacking. Attack broken up by Artillery barrage	
10.30 p.m.	Bombardment of our line became most greatly intensified, but the majority of shots fired were, very few fell on our trenches	

Army Form C. 2118.

WAR DIARY
or
INTELLIGENCE SUMMARY.
(Erase heading not required.)

83rd Dis R F A

Instructions regarding War Diaries and Intelligence Summaries are contained in F.S. Regs., Part II and the Staff Manual respectively. Title pages will be prepared in manuscript.

Hour, Date, Place	Summary of Events and Information	Remarks and references to Appendices
AUTHUILLE WOOD		
11 a.m. 15.10.16	Enemy again counter attacks, but again were driven off with great loss. During the attack some Germans approached our Lammerkopfs. Rifle fire was concentrated on & obtained relevant tavert. Germans did not reach our trenches. Situation quiet.	
noon 16.10.16		
3 p.m. to 5.30 p.m.	Enemy shelled trench areas heavily. During the night enemy shelled our trenches, no raid attempted.	
17.10.16	Owing to mass of infantry and front held by Bde, targets were selected near June. Wire cutting carried out on STUFF TRENCH prior to infantry attack.	
18.10.16	Enemy artillery very active. Our trenches and back area shelled. Our balloon fired on noticeably.	
19.10.16	Attack on STUFF TRENCH ordered for to day, postponed owing to bad weather. Enemy again shelling heavily.	
20.10.16	Attack on STUFF TRENCH ordered for 21st. Zero hour 12-6 h. Enemy shelled our front line & approaches heavily.	
5.30 a.m. 21.10.16	Enemy attacks SCHWABEN REDOUBT after heavy bombardment. They gained a footing but were ejected. Enemy about 50 strong our trenches and 35 prisoners including one Officer.	
12-6 p.m.	Our Infantry attacked STUFF and REGINA trenches. Our Artillery barrage at June. All objections were taken by 3 h.m. Enemy Artillery active during operations.	

Army Form C. 2118.

WAR DIARY
or
INTELLIGENCE SUMMARY.
(Erase heading not required.)

Instructions regarding War Diaries and Intelligence Summaries are contained in F.S. Regs., Part II. and the Staff Manual respectively. Title pages will be prepared in manuscript.

Hour, Date, Place	Summary of Events and Information	Remarks and references to Appendices
Authuille Wood		
22-10-16	Nothing to Report.	
23-10-16	Preparation firing made for further advance to River 17??? Batteries engaged were cutting and registering points	
24-10-16	" " "	
25-10-16	" " "	
26-10-16	" " "	
27-10-16	" " "	
28-10-16	" " "	
29-10-16	" " "	
30-10-16	" " "	
31-10-16	5.45 pm Enemy shelled our Lookout Post in Popes ???. Retaliation by Lewis & ????.	

H.A.Wilke 2/Lt. R.F.A.
for Lt Colonel
Commdg 53rd Bde R.F.A.

War Diary
for
November 1916

83rd Bde. R.F.A.

Army Form C. 2118.

Field Box PZ.9

WAR DIARY
or
INTELLIGENCE SUMMARY.
(Erase heading not required.)

Instructions regarding War Diaries and Intelligence Summaries are contained in F.S. Regs., Part II and the Staff Manual respectively. Title pages will be prepared in manuscript.

Hour, Date, Place	Summary of Events and Information	Remarks and references to Appendices
1. 10.11.16	Considerable aerial activity by our machines	
2. 10.11.16	Barrages as ordered in O.O.99 found to be unsatisfactory owing to ground charge of zone with 82nd Bde decided on	
3. 11.11.16	Amendments to O.O.99 with reference batteries issued. Registration of new zone completed. Enemy shelled road leading to batteries.	
4. 11.11.16	Hostile aerial activity. Nothing unusual.	
5. 11.11.16	Nothing unusual.	
6. 11.11.16	Zones exchanged with 82 RAB Bde at 12 noon. Enemy shelled our front line. Retaliation by heavies.	
7. 11.11.16	Hostile shelling during the night of Ancre Valley & back area. Enemy planes active during the night. Nothing to report.	
8. 11.11.16	Nothing to report.	
9. 11.11.16	Allied front areas shelled by high velocity gun. Considerable aerial activity at night.	
10. 11.11.16 5.45	Intense morning bombardment.	
11. 11.11.16 5.45	Bombardment of enemy's trenches as in O.O.100 "Z" day to be 13th November.	
12. 11.11.16 5.45	Bombardment of enemy's trenches with a 6" & 6"H. Enemy made his endeavour to make his cloud in mornings his par opéra. Very foggy all day. Intense bombardment throughout the day. Orders to effect that the operations detailed in O.O.99 would take place on Z day. First Stage (H) (M) Peace in stages.	

(73989) W4141-463. 400,000. 9/14. H.&J.Ltd. Forms/C. 2118/10.

Army Form C. 2118.

Bm Brigade R.F.A.

WAR DIARY
or
INTELLIGENCE SUMMARY.
(Erase heading not required.)

Hour, Date, Place	Summary of Events and Information	Remarks and references to Appendices
13th November 1916.	"Z" day. During night an intermittent fire was kept up by our artillery. This lasted until Zero hour when the artillery dropped on to its barrage. 5.45 am Zero hour. Weather very foggy. Our infantry left the trenches. All objectives were taken, and our infantry pushed along on the line of the River ANCRE. St Pierre DIVION fell into our hands and numerous prisoners were taken. Enemy guns on ZYMMA day were ennobated and preparations for a further advance were taken into hand. Barrages of fire were established during the night in support of infantry.	
Nov 14th 1916.	Quiet indication that attack will be continued on 14/15/16/1916. Batteries registration zones allotted to them. Retaliating fire on hostile batteries was also carried out.	
Nov 15th 1916.	The 39th Division was relieved by the 19th Division and E.W. Div. Artillery came under orders of the 19th Division.	
Nov 16/17 1916.	Attack on Grand Court Trench by 19th Division on front of ST PIERRE DIVION. Enemy shelled STUFF Trench, BLUE T and HANSA Line. Territorials fired bursts on enemy lines and shelter trenches on enemy tracks in retaliation.	

Army Form C. 2118.

WAR DIARY
or
INTELLIGENCE SUMMARY.
(Erase heading not required.)

Hrs Brigade R.F.A.

Instructions regarding War Diaries and Intelligence Summaries are contained in F.S. Regs., Part II. and the Staff Manual respectively. Title pages will be prepared in manuscript.

Hour, Date, Place	Summary of Events and Information	Remarks and references to Appendices
Nov 17th 1916. Nov 18/1916.	Nothing to report beyond usual artillery activity on both sides. Attack by 19th Division supported by this Div Art. Carried out. Zero hour 6.20 a.m. Barrage and lifts Carried out by batteries in support of infantry. DESIRE Trench was captured and many prisoners. Batteries established a barrage around GRANDCOURT where was kept up that night. Infantry soon made to counterattacks the ground taken on the evening of this day to assist in this. Batteries carried on almost steady fire on enemy approaches throughout the day. Enemy artillery fire was below normal. Nothing to report beyond ordinary night firing.	
Nov 19th 1916.		
Nov 20/1916.	Nothing to report during day. S.O.S at 5.30 p.m. Probably false alarm. Nothing happened in our sector beyond Bn commences work on O.P.	
Nov 21/1916		
Nov 22. 1916	Nothing to report.	
23.	nothing to report.	
24.	nothing to report.	

Army Form C. 2118.

WAR DIARY
or
INTELLIGENCE SUMMARY.
(Erase heading not required.)

53rd Brigade R.F.A.

Hour, Date, Place	Summary of Events and Information	Remarks and references to Appendices
Nov 25th 1916	writing report.	
" 26th "	have viewed to reorganisation of Brigades.	
" 27th "	have little reserved for itinerary to rest billets.	
Nov 28th 1916		
Nov 29th 1916	nothing to report	
Nov 30/1916		

H. A. Wolfe 2/12/9/12
for Lt-Col
Comm'g 53rd Bde R.F.A.

Vol 17

Confidential
War Diary of
83rd. Brigade, R.F.A.

From December 1st 1916. to December 31st 1916.

(Volume VI)

WAR DIARY
or
INTELLIGENCE SUMMARY.
(Erase heading not required.)

Army Form C. 2118.

Hour, Date, Place	Summary of Events and Information	Remarks and references to Appendices
1/12/16.	Nothing to report.	
2/12/16.	Batteries were entrained from the line and proceeded to wagon lines. Bre A.Cn were entrained at BOUZINCOURT. The Brigade was relieved by the 59th Brigade R.F.A.	
3/12/16.	A,B and C Batteries were formed into 6 gun batteries. Left Section of C Battery 85th Brigade R.F.A became Left Section A/83. Right Section of B — — — — — Left Section B/83. Left Section of D — — — — — Left Section C/83. The Brigade now consists of 3 Six Gun 18pr Batteries & one gun 4·5" How B4 and one Bde Hd Qrs.	
4/12/16.	The Brigade marched to AMPLIERS on route for Rest area. AMPLIERS was reached at 4·30 pm and the Brigade billeted there for the night.	
5/12/16.	The Brigade again took the road on route for CRAMONT. CRAMONT was reached at 3 pm and the Brigade billeted here for the night.	
6/12/16.	The Brigade left CRAMONT, for destination CAOURS, and reached at 2 pm. CAOURS was reached at 9am en route for 6/12/16.	

Army Form C. 2118.

WAR DIARY
or
INTELLIGENCE SUMMARY.
(Erase heading not required.)

Instructions regarding War Diaries and Intelligence Summaries are contained in F. S. Regs., Part II. and the Staff Manual respectively. Title pages will be prepared in manuscript.

Hour, Date, Place	Summary of Events and Information	Remarks and references to Appendices
7/12/16	The Brigade is now at rest at CAOURS.	
8/12/16	" "	
9/12/16	" "	
10/12/16	" "	
11/12/16		
12/12/16		
13/12/16		
14/12/16		
15/12/16		
16/12/16		
17/12/16		
18/12/16		
19/12/16		
20/12/16		
21/12/16		
22/12/16		
23/12/16	Orders received that 18th Div. Art. will proceed back to the line on 2/1/917. Nothing to report. Still in Rest.	

Army Form C. 2118.

WAR DIARY
or
INTELLIGENCE SUMMARY.
(Erase heading not required.)

Hour, Date, Place	Summary of Events and Information	Remarks and references to Appendices
24/12/16.	Brigade Training carried on.	
25/12/16.	Xmas Day. Holiday	
26/12/16.	Training carried on in Bos Area	
27/12/16.	"	
28/12/16.	"	
29/12/16.	"	
30/12/16.	"	
31/12/16.	"	

HSP White Lt Col
for Lt. Col. R.F.A.
Commanding Bam Brigade R.F.A.

83 Bde RFA
Vol 18

WAR DIARY
or
INTELLIGENCE SUMMARY.
(Erase heading not required.)

Army Form C. 2118.

Hour, Date, Place	Summary of Events and Information	Remarks and references to Appendices
January 1st 1917. 2nd 1917	Brigade prepared for the move back to forward area.	
	The Brigade marched off from CROUPS at 10am en route for BOUZINCOURT via BEALCOURT, GEZAINCOURT and SARTON. BEALCOURT was reached at 2pm and a halt was made for the night.	
3rd 1917	The Brigade left BEALCOURT at 9.30am and marched to GEZAINCOURT, reaching the latter place at 1pm where a halt was made for the night.	
4th 1917	The Brigade left GEZAINCOURT at 7.30am and marched to SARTON. SARTON was reached at 12 noon and the Brigade billetted there for the night.	
5th 1917	The Brigade marched off from SARTON at 7.30am and reached BOUZINCOURT at 1pm. Wagon Lines were established and Batteries relieved those prior to filling the guns up to the line. Brigade Head Quarters moved up to X 3 c. 15.40 and commenced making dug out etc for Bde Head Qr and Batteries in R 33 a.b.d. C Battery in X 3 a.	

Army Form C. 2118.

WAR DIARY
or
INTELLIGENCE SUMMARY.
(Erase heading not required.)

Instructions regarding War Diaries and Intelligence Summaries are contained in F.S. Regs., Part II and the Staff Manual respectively. Title pages will be prepared in manuscript.

Hour, Date, Place	Summary of Events and Information	Remarks and references to Appendices
6. 1. 17.	A/13 Batteries moved in with one section. Work continued on gun pits etc	
7. 1. 17.	A/13 Batteries moved in complete. O.P. one section each	
8. 1. 17.	All Batteries in the line. Brigade covering front of 306 Bde R&a 6th Div reinforcing it. Work continued on positions	
9. 1. 17.	O.O. 107 Received	
10. 1. 17.	O.O. 107 Carried out. Raid carried out by 6th Div. Zero hour 6.37 a.m.	
11. 1. 17.	Work continued on positions. Otherwise nothing to report	
12. 1. 17.	Nothing to report	
13. 1. 17.	Deadly movement of trench D/line receives	
14. 1. 17.	Boom Ravine & MIRAUMONT CEMETERY kept under fire of D/Me.	
15. 1. 17.	Nothing to report	
16. 1. 17.	O.O. 35 6.D in reserve.	
17. 1. 17.	Operations carried out as above. Zero hour 6.35	
18. 1. 17.	Nothing to report	

Army Form C. 2118.

WAR DIARY
or
INTELLIGENCE SUMMARY.
(Erase heading not required.)

Hour, Date, Place	Summary of Events and Information	Remarks and references to Appendices
19.1.17	Preparations made to take over from 61st Div Art. 83 Bev reunno on Cerisy subsector	
20.1.17	83 Bde takes over RyA subsector reputation completed	
21.1.17	10 am relief completed 83 Bde responsible for line 2.05 took over at 10.am S/W checking of Battery positions	
22.1.17	Batteries observing enemy lines and any causes or— targets of fire	
23.1.17	Nothing to report but normal bursts of fire on both sides.	
24.1.17	— " —	
25.1.17		
26.1.17		
27.1.17		
28.1.17		
29.1.17		
30.1.17		
31.1.17		

JMcOkeasra
Lt-Col
Commd 83rd Bde RFA

83rd

~~Bde~~ Bde R. F. A

Feb

8ol XIX

83rd Brigade
R.F.A.

WAR DIARY
or
INTELLIGENCE SUMMARY
(Erase heading not required.)

Army Form C. 2118

Place	Date	Hour	Summary of Events and Information	Remarks and references to Appendices
	1/2/17		Battery fired on enemy clothes and engaged parties seen in the open. At 5.15 a.m. Battery opened fire on S.O.S. lines in response to "S.O.S." and enemy's attempted raid was a complete failure. Enemy artillery was above normal.	
	2/2/17		Battery fired on enemy approaches and defences. Enemy shelled various points in our lines during the day.	
	3/2/17		Stop opened fire at 1.30 p.m. and opened a Barrage on GRAND COURT trench, lasting twenty minutes. In reply the enemy shelled Staff Resort.	
	4/2/17		3 enemy planes flew over battery position at 12.30 p.m. Battery fired on enemy approaches etc. Dump Ration being fired on BOOM RAVINE. A Barrage was placed on enemy's front system to assist 63rd Division in operation against PUISIEUX and River trenches. This objective was gained. An intense barrage was opened on all enemy approaches at 10.7 a.m. in response to "S.O.S.". This was continued until 11.30 a.m. Enemy artillery very active throughout the day. Enemy aeroplanes were also active behind our lines.	
	5/2/17		Part of the new left sub thought to the day on our position approaches to the PUISIEUX trench. A Barrage was placed on completion onto a mass or fellow trench. Enemy Artillery again active at the...	

WAR DIARY or INTELLIGENCE SUMMARY

Army Form C. 2118

Place	Date	Hour	Summary of Events and Information	Remarks and references to Appendices
	6/2/17		Usual programme of firing on enemy defences and approaches etc. Enemy Artillery was fairly active throughout the day. Enemy aeroplanes also active over our lines.	
	7/2/17		At 1-30 am a barrage was opened out 16 avril in an attack aimed against Totty Trench by 106 East Regt. No resistance was offered by the enemy and the trench was found to be unoccupied. Enemy reply to our barrage was feeble.	
	8/2/17		Enemy was reported to have evacuated GRANDCOURT. Our infantry occupied GRANDCOURT Trench on spur R6.a.75.65. Batteries carried out registration on various points and fired salvoes on selected points.	
	9/2/17		Enemy artillery very quiet. Nothing but occasional bursts of fire on enemy approaches. D/94 was split up and the left section of this Battery became the left section of D/93 thus forming D/93 into a 6 gun battery.	
	10/2/17		Nothing but spasmodic firing on hostile areas.	
	11/2/17		Programme of firing carried out on enemy approaches etc. Enemy Artillery fairly active.	

WAR DIARY
or
INTELLIGENCE SUMMARY

(Erase heading not required.)

Army Form C. 2118

Instructions regarding War Diaries and Intelligence Summaries are contained in F.S. Regs., Part II. and the Staff Manual respectively. Title Pages will be prepared in manuscript.

Place	Date	Hour	Summary of Events and Information	Remarks and references to Appendices
	12/2/17		The Brigade were relieved & took over new positions in rear to assist the Right Battalion of 10th Division. Brigade Head Quarters were established at P32 & T4 and batteries took up positions in R27c and R26c.	
	13/2/17		Batteries registered "zero" in front of South MIRAUMONT Trench and GRANDCOURT Trench in view of forthcoming operations. 18th Div. Art. O.O. 112 received. Enemy operations against strong points at R26a9-5 and R16 6-514 were to be carried out on the 14th & 15th Inst. Enemy artillery active throughout the day.	
	14/2/17		Minor operation of 18th Div. carried out as above, 106 prisoners being taken. Bosch of fire were carried out by batteries on enemy approaches etc. There was enemy artillery activity.	
	15/2/17		Action was taken on retaliation points by batteries. Batteries fired on S.O.S. lines at 6.40 pm. Wire cutting also carried out during the day.	
	16/2/17		A minor operation was carried out by our infantry, assisted by artillery at 5.45pm. Enemy artillery below normal. Wire cutting and also fire on enemy approaches etc. Steps prevented with "Wire cutting" and also fire on enemy approaches etc.	

WAR DIARY or INTELLIGENCE SUMMARY

Army Form C. 2118

Place	Date	Hour	Summary of Events and Information	Remarks and references to Appendices
	17/2/17		Shown never that 1916 Division letter together along will 63rd and 3rd Division the line EAST MIRAUMONT Road and various other enemy points. Zero hour 5:45am. A Barking barrage was opened at this time 6 mins starting impactly. All objectives were gained by 1916 Division and 63rd Div but the 3rd Division met with strong opposition from the enemy and did not gain their objective. Batterio kept up a heavy slow barrage the day 15 minutes' temporary Concentrations opening every Boom RAVINE and gaps N of Grandcourt Trench slung to the fact the enemy had been warned of our intended attack). A heavy barrage was opened by him on our front line prevents to our barrage but this absence of a good place when our barrage was commenced. Intense fire on enemy approaches and trenches to prevent him arriving reinforcements who were heavy casualties the ground taken from him the previous day. At 6:45am Btys opened fire on S.O.S. lines in response to an appeal from the Division on our left. Intense artillery was very active throughout the day. (The 55th Infantry Bde. relieves the 8th Inf. Bde.) Bursts of fire on enemy approaches etc. carried out by batteries.	
	18/2/17		Enemy artillery activity normal.	

Army Form C. 2118

WAR DIARY
or
INTELLIGENCE SUMMARY
(Erase heading not required.)

Place	Date	Hour	Summary of Events and Information	Remarks and references to Appendices
	20/2/17		Nothing but usual bursts of fire on both sides.	
	21/2/17		" " " " " "	
	22/2/17		" " " " " "	
	23/2/17		Enemy artillery fire below normal.	
	24/2/17		Nothing to report. Enemy has retired out of range of guns. Owing to bad state of ground, Batteries could not move forward. Nothing to report beyond reconnaissance carried out for means by which Batteries could be got up into action.	
	25/2/17			
	26/2/17			
	27/2/17			
	28/2/17		Wagon lines were moved from Senlis to THIEPVAL.	

H A White
for Lieut-Colonel
Commanding ??? Bde R.F.A.

Vol 20

War Diary
for
March 1917.

83rd Brigade R.F.A.

18th Divisional Artillery

WAR DIARY
or
INTELLIGENCE SUMMARY.
(Erase heading not required.)

Army Form C. 2118.

83rd Bde R.F.A.

Hour, Date, Place	Summary of Events and Information	Remarks and references to Appendices
1/3/17	Nothing to report.	
2/3/17	Batteries supported infantry raid took prisoners E. of BOOM RAVINE with exception of two 18pdr guns which had to be left in the more for the night. Remainder of guns got into position and dug in by morning.	
3/3/17	One 18 pdr more sunk, dug out easily in LOUPART WOOD.	
4/3/17	Batteries carried on registration on LOUPART WOOD. O.P. established from which a good view of IRLES, Resurrection Trench and GREVILLERS Trench. Grés te Beer. Enemy shelled Pys and Hill 130 with 15cm shell otherwise hostile artillery below normal.	
5/3/17	Russians repulsed on Resurrection Trench (very annoying). "D" Battery repulsed on IRLES Church. Enemy shelled BOOM Ravine and West MIRAUMONT Copse. Very little active activity.	
6/3/17	Batteries fired barrage on Resurrection Trench at 12.30 am to assist infantry in a minor operation. (18th Div. Art. OO.117) Batteries also did 'wire cutting' during the day. Enemy Batteries from near GRÉVILLERS shelled during the day.	
7/3/17	"A" Battery fired on RAVINE. "D" By fired on GRÉVILLERS trench. Enemy shelled Pys and back areas intermittently throughout the day.	

Army Form C. 2118.

Bde Hqrs R.F.A.

WAR DIARY
INTELLIGENCE SUMMARY.
(Erase heading not required.)

Hour, Date, Place	Summary of Events and Information	Remarks and references to Appendices
8/3/17	Batteries were engaged cutting wire and also firing on Grevillers and rampart of line. "D" Battery also fired on IRLES. Enemy artillery very active throughout day especially on 9/11 am along railway as far Regina trench.	
9/3/17	Batteries fired on enemy approaches etc. Wire cutting carried out, also searching fire between Achiet-le-Petit and Grevillers. D/93 shelled Grevillers Trench and IRLES. Enemy shelled MIRAUMONT – Serre Valley.	
10/3/17	18th Div. Arty O.O. 118 carries out. The operation consists of the attack and capture of GREVILLERS Trench and IRLES. Zero hour was 5:15am. A raking barrage was opened at 5:15am to support 8th Suffolk Regiment who took all their objectives. Wire cutting also carried on. "A" and "B" Batteries were ordered to move up and take former positions for purpose of wire cutting on. A/79 and C/78 were attached to the Brigade to assist in latter operations and they took over position vacated by "A" and "B" Batteries respectively. Enemy artillery below normal.	

Army Form C. 2118.

318 Brigade R.F.A.

WAR DIARY
or
INTELLIGENCE SUMMARY.
(Erase heading not required.)

Instructions regarding War Diaries and Intelligence Summaries are contained in F.S. Regs., Part II and the Staff Manual respectively. Title pages will be prepared in manuscript.

Hour, Date, Place	Summary of Events and Information	Remarks and references to Appendices
11/3/17	Night:- firing and harassing fire carried out. A/79 and C/78 checked Barrage lines. D/83 carried out bombardment of enemy defences. "A" and "B" Batteries precaution wire cutting. Enemy shells now being into Irles. Six enemy planes flew out practising at 10.30 am. One of these was brought down and fell behind Bapaume Wood.	
12/3/17	Enemy reported to have evacuated the Rocquigny - Bihucourt Line. "A" and "B" Batteries fired on enemy tracks etc. Enemy artillery normal. Patrols reconnoitred for forward move.	
13/3/17 14/3/17 15/3/17 16/3/17	One section A/83 moved up into action near Irles. Nothing to report.	
17/3/17	Brigade moved up to positions between Silos and the Loupart Wood. Enemy shelled vicinity of Pys and Irles throughout the day. A/79 and C/78 were placed under orders of 176 Bde. A.A. A/83 fired on machine guns and working party in gists. Enemy evacuated Achiet-le-Petit - Bapaume Line.	
18/3/17	Nothing to report. Major Weyman reconnaissance carried out and Weyman twice moved up to be near Irles.	

WAR DIARY
INTELLIGENCE SUMMARY
(Erase heading not required.)

Army Form C. 2118

7th Brigade R.F.A.

Place	Date	Hour	Summary of Events and Information	Remarks and references to Appendices
IRLES	19/3/17		The Brigade received news to move up to MORY and assist the 7th Battery in the capture of ST LEGER-ST-MAIN. A start was made at 6 pm and Brigade moved to BIHUCOURT and IRLES for the night.	
	20/3/17		Advice received that the 18th Division secured to withdraws no Brigade left BIHUCOURT and retained to wagon lines near IRLES (G32c).	
	21/3/17		Nothing to report.	
	22/3/17			
	23/3/17			
	24/3/17		The Brigade marched to SENLIS and rested there for a day or two.	
	25/3/17			
	26/3/17		Nothing to report.	
	27/3/17		Brigade left SENLIS at 7.30 am and marched to RUBEMPRÉ where a halt was made for the night.	
	28/3/17		Brigade left RUBEMPRÉ at 8.30 am and marched to BEAUVAL and billeted there for the night.	
	29/3/17		Brigade left BEAUVAL at 9.30 am and marched to DOMLEGER for the night. Billets were later on and the Brigade rested for the night.	
	29/3/17		The Brigade left DOMLEGER and marched to HEUCHIN	
	30/3/17		The Brigade marched from Gonehy to Heuchin	
	31/3/17		The Brigade left Heuchin and marched to WITTERNESSE and rested there for the night.	

J.K. Dwike Lieut Col
Commdg 7th Bde R.F.A.

Vol 21

War Diary
of
April. 1917

83rd Brigade
R.F.A.

WAR DIARY
or
INTELLIGENCE SUMMARY

Army Form C. 2118

Place	Date	Hour	Summary of Events and Information	Remarks and references to Appendices
	1/4/17		The Brigade left WITTERNASSE and marched to MORBECQUE via AIRE. MORBECQUE was reached at 2pm and billets taken up. Was in First Army Area. The Brigade carried on a Training Programme.	
	7/4/17	7h/4/17	The One along with the 18th Division Artillery received that the B.E.F.R.A. ammunition cases were to be near the Base on the 18th inst.	
	18/4/17		The Brigade turned out at 9.30am but owing to the bad state of the weather, the inspection was cancelled.	
	19/4/17 to 23/4/17		Training proceeded with. Nothing else to report.	
	23/4/17		Orders received that Brigade along with Division (18th) moves to transferred to VII Corps and moves from MORBECQUE on the 24th April.	
	24/4/17		The Brigade left MORBECQUE at 9am and marched to BELLERIVE en route Rest. For the 3rd Army Area. Brigade arrived at BELLERIVE at 1pm and rested for the night 26th inst.	
	25/4/17		The Brigade left BELLERIVE next marched to ALLOUAGNE, leaving there for the night.	
	26/4/17		Brigade left ALLOUAGNE and marched to HEUCHIN again halted for the night	
	27/4/17		HEUCHIN was left at 9am and the Brigade marched to MACNICOURT via Couches via St Pol, again halting for the night.	

Army Form C. 2118

WAR DIARY
or
INTELLIGENCE SUMMARY
(Erase heading not required.)

Instructions regarding War Diaries and Intelligence Summaries are contained in F. S. Regs., Part II. and the Staff Manual respectively. Title Pages will be prepared in manuscript.

Place	Date	Hour	Summary of Events and Information	Remarks and references to Appendices
	29/4/17		The Bde left MAGNICOURT at 9am and marched to Aubigny area nr WANNY near ARRAS. The Brigade Bivouacked & there for the night	
	30/4/17		At 9am marched to wagon lines near BOISLEUX - ST AAPC reaching there about 11am. At 6pm Batteries went up into action in area about N 29 a and c. (Map Ref E 7 & R Plans).	

Mockte
Lieut. R.F.A.
Lieut Col
Comdy Bde R.F.A.

18th Divr

War Diary
for
MAY. 1917.

83rd Brigade
R.F.A.

Army Form C. 2118

65th Brigade R.F.A.

WAR DIARY
or
INTELLIGENCE SUMMARY
(Erase heading not required.)

Place	Date	Hour	Summary of Events and Information	Remarks and references to Appendices
Héninel	1/5/17		Forward Obs. posts sent up from wagon lines & to positions near HÉNINEL	Troop Reference E76 B9898
			Battery registered zone etc.	
			Enemy shelled HÉNINEL and surrounding ground, throughout the day.	
"	2/5/17		" " " " "	
"	3/5/17		18th Div. Art. OO. 132 received.	
			The 18" Div with 14" Div on right were to attack the German positions in front of CHERISY via the SENSÉE valley. 53rd Bde forming a lifting barrage in front of the attacking Battalions of 53rd & 54th Inf. Bdes with a stationary Vickers gun barrage. The attack was carried out in two stages. The attack commenced at 3.45" am on 3rd. The Capt. Bde. reached its objective having suffered moderate loss on return. M.G. fire. The Artillery barrage according to Infantry reports was very effective. During the early morning a heavy counter attack from the left flank of a Capt. number 30m from twelve Protector Barrage was kept up beyond the final objective opposite any were still and is still being beyond the village. At 7.15 am an attack was made on our right to enable us to take further to withdraw. This was very successful on the right flank but so on the left. Eventually our troops retreated to their old front line which they now hold as before. This proved to be a false alarm to an SOS. Box opened the rest of the night was comparatively quiet.	
"	4/5/17		Batteries harassing fire on enemy positions and approaches. Enemy shelling vicinity of HÉNINEL throughout the day from direction of VIS en ARTOIS aeroplanes of both sides very active.	
"	5/5/17	10.30pm	Harass harassing fire carried out. Batteries fired on "S.O.S." lines in reply to heavy barrage put on front line by the enemy. No infantry action started.	
"	6/5/17		Nothing but usual burst of fire on enemy positions and night forms. Enemy Artillery fire below normal.	

WAR DIARY or INTELLIGENCE SUMMARY

Army Form C. 2118

(Erase heading not required.)

Instructions regarding War Diaries and Intelligence Summaries are contained in F.S. Regs., Part II. and the Staff Manual respectively. Title Pages will be prepared in manuscript.

Place	Date	Hour	Summary of Events and Information	Remarks and references to Appendices
HÉNINEL	7/5/17		Btys carried out usual night and harassing fires.	
--"--	8/5/17		Enemy shelled COJEUL VALLEY intermittently throughout the day.	
--"--	9/5/17		Nothing to report but usual shelling by both sides. Batteries fire on enemy working parties.	
--"--	10/5/17		Enemy artillery normal. House shelling of HÉNINEL and surrounding vicinity.	
--"--	11/5/17		Btys carried out harassing fire on enemy front. "A" Bty switches to wagon lines to fire in this period of Rest. Wagon lines were leaving Ahiert as horses Guide track to BOIS St MARTIN. B.C. and D Btys fired on enemy working parties and Germans seen in the open. Enemy shelled vally between HÉNINEL and WANCOURT fairly heavily.	
--"--	12/5/17		Btys shelled enemy positions and carried out Registrations. D/83 shelled enemy dug out and CHÉRISY. They also registered with ar V29 a 7. Enemy fire below normal.	
--"--	13/5/17		Balloons were up most of the day. B.C. and D. Batteries fired on Germans seen in open. "B" Bty obtain FONTAINE Trench and CHÉRISY LYNE at intervals throughout the day. Slight shelling of COJEUL VALLEY by the Enemy but otherwise quiet.	
--"--	14/5/17		Batteries fired on parties seen in the open and with S.O.S. lines. 18/13 fired at respective O.P. at O32 a.F.9. Enemy shelled HÉNINEL and COJEUL VALLEY at intervals throughout the day.	

Army Form C. 2118

53rd Brigade R.F.A.

WAR DIARY or INTELLIGENCE SUMMARY

(Erase heading not required.)

Instructions regarding War Diaries and Intelligence Summaries are contained in F. S. Regs, Part II. and the Staff Manual respectively. Title Pages will be prepared in manuscript.

Place	Date	Hour	Summary of Events and Information	Remarks and references to Appendices
Héninel	15/5/17		Batteries carried out usual harassing fire on CHERISY and enemy positions. Enemy Artillery very active throughout the right and day. COTORI VALLEY, HENINEL and surrounding ground being heavily shelled with guns of all calibre. D/53 had 3 guns practically destroyed and has to be withdrawn to the wagon line.	
-"-	16/5/17		'B' and 'C' Batteries fired on S.O.S. lines and CHERISY at intervals throughout the day. Enemy Artillery not so active. COTORI VALLEY hung very shortly shelled during the morning.	
-"-	17/5/17		'B' and 'C' Batteries fired on Enemy parties and carried out harassing fire. Enemy shelled HENINEL and BG position heavily about dusk. Leander. 'A' Battery moved up into action into its position.	
-"-	18/5/17		181st Div. Arr. O.O. 123 received. Batteries carried out usual night firing and bursts of fire. Parties seen in the open also fired on. Enemy snipers a few shells in HENINEL and N39a. Quiet otherwise normal.	
-"-	19/5/17		Enemy artillery very active throughout day shelling ground and batteries around HENINEL. Our Batteries carried out usual harassing fire and shelled parties seen in the open.	

1875 Wt. W593/826 1,000,000 4/15 J.B.C. & A. A.D.S.S./Forms/C. 2118.

Army Form C. 2118

WAR DIARY
INTELLIGENCE SUMMARY
(Erase heading not required.)

83rd Brigade R.F.A.

Place	Date	Hour	Summary of Events and Information	Remarks and references to Appendices
HONNECOURT	20/9/17	At 5.10am	The division on our right attacked the HINDENBURG line in vic. The Couts on our right attacking at the same time further south. The attack was partially successful. The 18 Div Art. attacked Bon Bavery the enemy's defences in front of CHERISY with a view to inflicting casualties. Infantry attacks were made. Batteries sniped ground East of CHERISY during the afternoon, inflicted undoubted casualties on enemy reinforcements coming up towards FONTAINE WOOD.	E. TERRIGNY sheet.
"	21/5/17	At 6pm	Bdy reached position Nth over previous lines by 148th Brigade. Bde Hd Qrs moves to T.S.c.5.9 and took over from H.Q. 148 Brigade. The regiments of this Brigade passed over to 83rd Brigade at 8pm. Bdy now in action as follows. "A" - T.4.d 75.75. "B" - T.4.a.2.8. "C". 74 to 75.05. T.om = U.1.c.o-8 to U.1.b.8.3.	
"	22/5/17		Enemy Artillery normal. Batteries Registered New Zones.	
"	23/5/17		Enemy artillery below normal.	
"	24/5/17		Nothing but minor bursts of fire on both sides	

Army Form C. 2118

WAR DIARY
or
INTELLIGENCE SUMMARY
(Erase heading not required.)

Instructions regarding War Diaries and Intelligence Summaries are contained in F.S. Regs., Part II. and the Staff Manual respectively. Title Pages will be prepared in manuscript.

Place	Date	Hour	Summary of Events and Information	Remarks and references to Appendices
COTEUL VALLEY	25/9/17	—	Batteries carried on usual harassing fire. 'D' Battery kept wagon line but moved into action at N.34.b.6.3. Enemy shelled CONCRETE Trench and tank area intermittently.	Itinerary on map. S/12 B.
	26/9/17	10.24p	Enemy aeroplane dropped 12 bombs in T.10 & Usual Artillery fire on both sides. A/83 withdrew from position and moved 18th Div. Art. O.O. 184 received. to wagon line for short period of rest.	
	27/9/17		O.O. 124 Carried out. 18th Div. Art. action covered with 33rd Division in the of Tunnel Trench between SENSEE River and PLUM Trench. Zero hour was 1.55pm. A/83 batteries barraged YORK Trench (V1.d.0.5 to U.6.7.1). D/83 barraged M.Gs at U.b.5.1 and V.1.a.2.9. Right Brigade fired. The Left Brigade reached its objective with ease too. Rifles were infested in enemy parties seen During the afternoon many casualties were inflicted on enemy parties seen in the open. At 2–10pm a German Counter Attack attempted to cross over the open was engaged by C/83 and airplanes.	
	28/9/17		Enemy planes & heavy barrage was kept down and was very active throughout the day. Batteries fired usual tasks and harassing fire. Several enemy parties seen in the open were fired on and casualties inflicted. Top band OK was leaving shells at intervals throughout the day.	

Army Form C. 2118

WAR DIARY
or
INTELLIGENCE SUMMARY
(Erase heading not required.)

53rd Brigade R.F.A.

Instructions regarding War Diaries and Intelligence Summaries are contained in F.S. Regs., Part II. and the Staff Manual respectively. Title Pages will be prepared in manuscript.

Place	Date	Hour	Summary of Events and Information	Remarks and references to Appendices
COTEAU WOOD	29/5/17		Batteries carried out harassing fire on enemy positions and working parties. Enemy Shelled Battery positions with occasional rounds during day.	Trench Map
—	30/5/17		Nothing to report. Usual shelling on both sides.	
—	31/5/17		Gas shell bombardment carried out by D/53. All Batteries fired on enemy parties seen in the open at 11.30 am Up to S.O.S. action. At 12.30 am and Batteries opened out for 20 minutes. Enemy shelled Two 75 a and N 3 r with guns of all calibres and also gas shells.	

[signature] Lieut. R.F.A.
for Lieut. Colonel
Commdg. 53rd Brigade R.F.A.

1875 Wt. W593/826 1,000,000 4/15 J.B.C. & A. A.D.S.S./Forms/C. 2118.

8 Bde. Bde.
R. F. A.

June 1917

Army Form C. 2118.

WAR DIARY
INTELLIGENCE SUMMARY
(Erase heading not required.)

8th Brigade R.F.A.

Hour, Date, Place	Summary of Events and Information	Remarks and references to Appendices
June 1st 1917	Battери fire on enemy parties seen in open.	See Operns Maps.
	12.30am In reply to Enemy heavy put on our front line Batteries fired on S.O.S. lines for twenty minutes. D/83 carried out a pro programme of enemy (Westmoreland?) enemy artillery very active shelling and all address back for shelter.	
June 2/17	Nomal shelling on both sides.	
June 3/17	Batteries carried out harassing fire on enemy frontline Enemy artillery very active. Back area shelled by gas shells.	
June 4/17	Batteries fired on enemy battalion seen in the open. Enemy artillery of enemy artillery	
June 5/17	'G' Battery moved up into the line. Batteries shelled enemy positions and parties seen in the open. Enemy artillery very active.	
June 6/17	C/63 arrived into dug outs at VII Corps Res Camp. X7a. Some shelling on both sides.	
June 7/17	Nothing to report.	
June 8/17	S.O.S. received at 12.7 midnight but Shelling on trench areas.	
June 9/17	S.O.S. received at 12.7 midnight and batteries fired a barrage for half an hour. Nothing to report.	

WAR DIARY or INTELLIGENCE SUMMARY

Army Form C. 2118.

Hour, Date, Place	Summary of Events and Information	Remarks and references to Appendices
11/9/17	Nothing to report.	
12/9/17	""	
13/9/17	Batteries fired on patrols seen in the open. Enemy artillery very quiet.	
14/9/17	Batteries carried out shoots. Harassing fire. Enemy shelled Battery position fairly heavily from 2:30pm to 5:30pm.	Map 57B S.W.
15/9/17	Nothing much happened in our sector. Artillery fire on Enemy positions to assist II Corps. Enemy slightly more active with artillery.	
16/9/17	13th Div. Art. O.O. 125 carried out. The 21st Div. in conjunction with 57th Division was to explain the HINDENBURG Support line from M42 H9-M5 to M7 b4-2. To assist in this attack "A" Bty. passed a barrage on BUCKCOURT Rd., "B" Bty. on FONTAINE- "C" Bty. on VALLEY "D" in USA on M St. Zero hour was 3:10am. This attack was particularly successful. "C" Bty moves into action from VII Corps Res Camp. "D" Bty. left position and went into action at VII Corps Res Camp.	
17/9/17	"C" Bty fired SOS line at 12 noon. Nothing else to report. Fairly quiet.	

Army Form C. 2118.

WAR DIARY
or
INTELLIGENCE SUMMARY.
(Erase heading not required.)

Instructions regarding War Diaries and Intelligence Summaries are contained in F.S. Regs., Part II and the Staff Manual respectively. Title pages will be prepared in manuscript.

Hour, Date, Place	Summary of Events and Information	Remarks and references to Appendices
18/4/17	Very quiet Day. Units harassing fire carries on. 16th Div. Arty H.Q. went into rest and Brigade was attached to 50th Div. Art.	
19/4/17	Harassing fire carries out. Enemy Artillery quiet.	
20/4/17	Nothing to report	
21/4/17	D. Battery carries out a gas shell bombardment.	
22/4/17	Nothing to report	
23/4/17	"A" "B" and "D" Batteries moved out of action. "C" Battery establish at BOIRY ST RICTRUDE	
24/4/17		
25/4/17		
26/4/17		
27/4/17	"A" "C" and "D" Batteries left corps Rest camp.	
28/4/17	Proceeded to VII Corps Rest Camp.	
29/4/17	— " — Nothing to report.	
30/4/17	— " —	
31/4/17	— " —	

C.R. Crouch, March 9/1/
Lieut-Colonel R.F.A.
Commanding 82nd Brigade R.F.A.

18th Div. R.E. A.D.
August 1917
WD 23

Army Form C. 2118

WAR DIARY
or
INTELLIGENCE SUMMARY
(Erase heading not required.)

Place	Date	Hour	Summary of Events and Information	Remarks and references to Appendices
Dickebusch	1st August 1917		In the attack on the Ypres front on July 31st Advanced D.H.Q. were at Dickebusch remainder of H.Q. at Renninghelst. On August 4th the Division relieved the 30th Div. and took over Canal Reserve Camp at Dickebusch. In its new fortnight the work chiefly consisted in consolidating such high ground as had been gained in the fighting of the 31st July, and the repairing and laying forward tracks in the devastated area to the front line. As the relief of the Division seemed imminent effort was made to fill two forward ways of approach (find walks) and these were laid before being relieved of the 56th Div. On the 13th & 14th the 79th Bgd. remained in the sector until 2 Bgd. til the 18th to complete advanced strong point and on the 19th arrived at R.E. area. Remainder of unit detailed to R.E. and Divisional Casualties to officers Ambulance & an Killed 392 o.r. to Casualties to V.O.R's been light considering the amount of work which was done in the forward area.	

Shafer Capt R.E.
Adjutant 18th Div. R.E.

Army Form C. 2118.

WAR DIARY
INTELLIGENCE SUMMARY.
(Erase heading not required.)

Instructions regarding War Diaries and Intelligence Summaries are contained in F.S. Regs., Part II and the Staff Manual respectively. Title pages will be prepared in manuscript.

VIII Corps
53rd Brigade R.F.A.

Hour, Date, Place	Summary of Events and Information	Remarks and references to Appendices
Sept 1st 1917	Brigade in Rest in the OUDEZEELE area serving the 1st Division Artillery	"HAZEBROUCK" map
Sept 2nd 1917	Training and refitting commenced.	
Sept 3/1917	II Corps Commander inspected the Brigade (serving with 1st Div Art) and presented Meid Ribbons	
Sept 4/1917 to Sept 20/1917	Nothing to report.	
Sept 21/1917	Brigade marches from OUDEZEELE to SERQUES.	
Sept 22/1917 6	Brigade resting in SERQUES.	
Sept 24/1917		
Sept 25/1917	Brigade left SERQUES and marched ERINGHEM and came under the orders of XVIII Corps.	
Sept 26/1917	Brigade marches from ERINGHEM to surgeon lines near POPERINGHE	

WAR DIARY

INTELLIGENCE SUMMARY
(Erase heading not required.)

83rd Brigade R.F.A.

Army Form C. 2118.

Hour, Date, Place	Summary of Events and Information	Remarks and references to Appendices
Sept 27/9/17	Batteries took over guns in the line from 241st Brigade R.F.A. 83rd and 84th Brigades are now in the line and form Centre Group of 58 K Divisional Artillery. Relief complete by 3pm. Brigade Hd Qrs took over from 241st Bde at 11.0d TOP Farm. Centre Group came under the orders of 58 K.D.A. Supervision.	Ref Map ST JULIEN 28 NW2
Sept 28/9/17	Line covered is D1d.90.50 to D.1.c.70.35. S.O.S. signal lit at 6pm. Registration was carried out.	
Sept 29/9/17	Centre Group was under the orders of 86 D.V. Art. Normal programme of harassing fire carried on.	
Sept 30/9/17	Bursts of fire were employed this evening as Enemy artillery very active.	
	Casualties. Major S.J. Samuels killed in action. 29/9/17 2/Lt W.J. Rotheram ——"—— 2/Lt A.J. Dobson wounded in action. 28/9/17 5 Killed other Ranks 18 wounded and wounded.	

W.B. Cruickshank Capt r.f.a
for Lt Col R.F.A
83rd Bde R.F.A

Commanding 83rd Bde R.F.A

18TH DIVISIONAL ARTILLERY.

83RD BRIGADE, R.F.A.

WAR DIARY

- FOR -

MONTH OF OCTOBER, 1917.

Army Form C. 2118.

WAR DIARY
— of —
INTELLIGENCE SUMMARY.
(Erase heading not required.)

Instructions regarding War Diaries and Intelligence Summaries are contained in F.S. Regs., Part II and the Staff Manual respectively. Title pages will be prepared in manuscript.

8th Brigade R.F.A.

Hour, Date, Place	Summary of Events and Information	Remarks and references to Appendices
ST JULIEN AREA 1/10/17	Brigade in action covering the Pole Cappelle area under the orders of 48th Div. Arty.	Map Reference St. Julien Sheet 28NW2
2/10/17 3/10/17 4/10/17	Harassing fire carried out on enemy lines.	
5/10/17	Barrage in accordance with 48th Div. Art. O.O. no 291 carried out. All objectives taken. Bursts of fire carried out by Batteries.	
6/10/17	C/53 and D/53 moved forward to new positions. Bursts of fire carried out on VACHER FARM. Harassing fire also carried out.	
7/10/17	Command of Group Zone handed over to 51st Bde. So Battery positions in SPRINGFIELD – WINNIPEG area handed over. Personnel of Bde. Brigade moved to wagon lines.	
8/10/17	Brigade came under the orders of 11th Divisional Artillery. Conference at 11th D.A. H.Q.	
9/10/17 10/10/17 11/10/17	Batteries moved into action in the Poelcappelle Rd. Personnel of all Batteries settled to wagon lines. Concern of Batteries attempted to get but owing to mechanism failure, they were not able to open fire.	

(73989) W4141—463. 400,000. 9/14. H.&J.Ltd. Forms/C. 2118/10.

WAR DIARY

INTELLIGENCE SUMMARY

Army Form C. 2118.

Bn. Bnyeun [?]

Hour, Date, Place	Summary of Events and Information	Remarks and references to Appendices
12/10/17	Bde HQr at wagon line. Batteries in action but not against enemy to fire.	
13/10/17	Bn Bde relieves 545 Bde and took over the line at CAME POST (eg a 6.2). Col Bingham took over Command of 'A' Group. N.815 Div Arty. '7' Group comprises 8 Bde (silent) 256th Bde. no followers.	
14/10/17	Potomac of Bn Batteries at wagon lines resting.	
15/10/17	Nothing to report	
19/10/17	1614 Bde relieves 256th Bde and came under orders of '7 Group'.	
20/10/17	Bombardment tasks by 256th Bde carried out.	
21/10/17	Bn personnel of Batteries returns to gun positions	
22/10/17	1615 Div Art. O.O. No. 130 carries out operations 5.30pm Enemy Grand up on a very successful. SOS Fire An Erickle attack. This gun broken up by fire on SOS line and M.G. fire from MEUNIER mine.	
23/10/17	Nothing to report	
24/10/17	Bombardments as per 1815 SAA Group Order No 12 carried out. Hostile Battery at V.10.6.9.5 engaged.	
25/10/17	Bombardment tasks and harassing fire carried out.	

Army Form C. 2118.

53rd Bde R.F.A

WAR DIARY
or
INTELLIGENCE SUMMARY.
(Erase heading not required.)

Hour, Date, Place	Summary of Events and Information	Remarks and references to Appendices
25/10/17 (continued)	Command of 18th Div. Art. Front handed over to C.R.A 58th D.A. Enemy apparently slipped away during the night and any 58th D.A. over no 1 & 2 Corner of Objectives (priority taken) & Hostile Batteries engaged were S.O.S. replies to at 5.30 p.m.	
26/10/17	3 Hostile Batteries engaged at 12.30 p.m, 2.40 p.m and 4 p.m, 60 rounds being fired on each.	
27/10/17	A Group was turned to 5th Corps and came under orders of C.R.A 63rd (RN) Division for tactical purposes. Nothing to report. Batteries silent.	
28/10/17	63rd RN. D.A. order no 127 carries out. Not considered a proceeding. After completing Barrage the Group moved to old Zone under orders of 58th D.A	
29/10/17		
30/10/17		
31/10/17	Nothing to report.	

Army Form C. 2118.

WAR DIARY
INTELLIGENCE SUMMARY.
(Erase heading not required.)

83rd Brigade RFA

Hour, Date, Place / Summary of Events and Information	Remarks and references to Appendices
Casualties during mnth. 1/Lieut- H.G. Deer wounded. Oct. 1917 2/Lieut- Wood wounded Oct- 21/10/1917. 2/Lieut- Roy Taylor wounded 23/10/17. (died of wounds 24/10/17) Lieut- J.R. Denny wounded 17/10/17. 2/Lieut- Barker killed in action 25/10/17. 2/Lieut- Cooper wounded 25/10/17 2/Lieut- Anyone wounded 27/10/17 Lieut- Stephenson wounded ? killed in action 16 N.C.Os and men wounded. 53	
	A.J. Burkhardt Capt. for Lt. Col. R.F.A. Commdg. 83rd Bde R.F.A.

Army Form C. 2118.

WAR DIARY
or
INTELLIGENCE SUMMARY
(Erase heading not required.)

83rd Brigade R.F.A.

Hour, Date, Place	Summary of Events and Information	Remarks and references to Appendices
July 12th 1917	Brigade H.Qrs at CANE POST (c9a6-2). Batteries in action in H.20.b.	PINEAPPLE
Nov 2nd 1917		
3-11-17	Harassing fire carried out as per 58th D.A. orders. Intermittent shelling of Battery areas by the enemy. Nothing but.	
4-11-17	-do- -do- -do-	
5-11-17	Batteries took part in Fifth Army Barrage and Bombardment of enemy positions at 4.40am.	(58th D.A. HQ 57)
6-11-17	Preliminary Bombardment opened at 4.50am. Creeping Barrage carried out by Batteries in support of an attack by the Canadian Corps on first of PASSCHENDAELE. Zero hour 6am. Burst of fire on enemy approaches during night.	58th DA OO 57
7-11-17	Army Barrage carried out at 5.30am. Rocket Barrage carried out at 1pm.	58th DA OO 58 58th DA OO 59.
8-11-17	Preparatory Barrage for future operations carried out at 4.15am and 5am. Enemy columns of infantry seen on N.W. of WESTROOSEBEKE.	58th DA OO 60.

(73989) W4141—463. 400,000. 9/14. H.&J.Ltd. Forms/C. 2118/10.

Army Form C. 2118.

WAR DIARY
or
INTELLIGENCE SUMMARY.
(Erase heading not required.)

3rd Brigade R.F.A.

Hour, Date, Place	Summary of Events and Information	Remarks and references to Appendices
Nov 9th 1917	1 Corps Preparatory Barrage carried out at 4-20 am Army Barrage carried out at 6 am day and night firing on enemy tracks carried out.	58 B D.A.O. 64
Nov 10th 1917 "D" Day	Batteries fired an enfilade Barrage at 6-5 am in support of an attack by the 131st Infantry Division	J/10 Div. O.O. No.?
Nov 11th 1917 "E" Day	Army Barrage carried out at 5 am All Batteries fired when called for CRA 1st Div. for SOS calls. Harassing fire only carried out. Secretly checking by the enemy.	58 B D.A.O. 66.
Nov 12th 1917 "F" Day	Army and Corps Barrages carried out. Bursts of fire on 101st Division in anticipation of a Counter attack. SOS replied to at 4-15 pm and 5-20 pm Preparatory Barrages and Harassing fire carried out.	58 B D.A.O. 68.
Nov 13th 1917 "G" Day		
Nov 14th 1917 "H" Day	Harassing fire carried on Secretly shelling by the enemy.	
Nov 15th 1917 "I" Day		
Nov 16th 1917 "J" Day	Nothing but the usual bursts of fire and Barrages.	

WAR DIARY or INTELLIGENCE SUMMARY

Army Form C. 2118.

B. n. Brigade R.F.A.

Hour, Date, Place	Summary of Events and Information	Remarks and references to Appendices
Nov 17th 1917.	16.15 Brigade took over the Command of "D" Group and were attached to 101st Division. Two Batteries of "D" Bn. R.F.A. came under of "D" Group. The Command of the 58th Div Art. Group passed to the C.R.A. 185 Div.	
Nov 18th 1917.	Minor harassing fire carried out. Batteries now under Command of the 185 Div. Art. Hostile Battery engaged at V/16.b.92.34. firing 250 rds - in front of the 355 Division. Hostile Battery engaged at 4pm. D/175 engaged Hostile Battery at- V/16.b.92.34. firing 250 rds -	
Nov 19/11/17	Minor harassing fire carried out.	
Nov 20/11/17	Very Quiet Day	
Nov 21/11/17	Nothing but intermittent Desultory on both sides.	
Nov 24/11/17	Hostile Bty. V.B. 74 engaged at 10.30am. Conc. Concentration Shoot Carried out at 4.15pm. Conc. Concentration Shoots carried out at 5.10am and 3.35pm	18½ B.T.A O.O. 22.
Nov 24/11/17	Heavy night-firing carried out on two pts enemy relief.	
Nov 24/11/17	Concentration shoot carried out at 5.20pm and minor harassing fire.	18½ B.T.A O.O. 23.
Nov 25/11/17.	"Defensive" PASCHENDAELE fire 7.30pm to 7.50pm. Minor night-firing.	

(73989) W4141—463. 400,000. 9/14. H.&J.Ltd. Forms/C. 2118/10.

Army Form C. 2118.

WAR DIARY
~~INTELLIGENCE SUMMARY~~
(Erase heading not required.)

83rd Brigade RFA

Hour, Date, Place	Summary of Events and Information	Remarks and references to Appendices
Nov 26/1917	Concentration Shoot carried out at 5.10 a.m.	
Nov 27/1917	H.Q. 82nd Bde RFA relieved H.Q. 83rd Bde at CAME POST and took over command of 17. Group 18th Div. Artr. Bde HQ established at TROIS TOURS. C. Battery moved to wagon lines for rest. D. Battery moved to wagon lines for rest.	
Nov 29/1917	A' and B' Batteries remain in action under orders of 82nd Bde RFA	
Nov 30/1917	Nothing to report. Casualties during mnth. Lieut Barthlement Jeuneusse 18.11.17. Lieut Leadbetter wounded 20.11.17). 8 men killed 7 men wounded.	

W.R Cruickshank Major
Lieut. Col. RFA
Comdg 83rd Brigade RFA

WAR DIARY
or
INTELLIGENCE SUMMARY.
(Erase heading not required.)

Army Form C. 2118.

(18th Divn)

8383ee B7a

Vol 29

Hour, Date, Place	Summary of Events and Information	Remarks and references to Appendices
Dec 1st 1917	Brigade H.Q. at TROIS TOURS Chateau near BRIELIN. A & B Batteries in action on the POELCAPPELLE ROAD under orders of 62 Bde B7a. C and D Batteries resting at Froyan Lines. Nothing to report.	
" 2d "		
" 3d "		
" 4th "		
" 5th "	C/83 went into action and relieved B/83	
" 6th "	Nothing to report	
" 7th "		
" 8th "		
" 9th "		
" 10th "	Batteries withdrew to Froyan Lines. Brigade marched from BRIELIN into rest area at CROMBEKE	
" 11th "	Nothing to report. Brigade in rest at CROMBEKE	
" 12th "		
Dec 13th "	Brigade took over from 234th Bde Brigade HQ in Hut as U.26.c.2.0 sheet 20 1/40000	
31 " "	Battery in action at U.21 e 8 3 × Rhun or Rhu 82
Dec 31st	C " " U.21 e 6.5 Bde B7cii
	D " " U.20 e 7-9.3
	Brigade remain at BDO M.BENE until the January 1918 nothing during month. 2 ORs killed	

Army Form C. 2118.

53rd Brigade R.F.A.

WAR DIARY
or
INTELLIGENCE SUMMARY.
(Erase heading not required.)

Hour, Date, Place	Summary of Events and Information	Remarks and references to Appendices
January 10th 1918.	January Items with the Brigade in action as follows:-	
	Hd Qrs. WOOD SRHO	
	"A" Battery U.26.c.2-0	
	"B" — U.21.d.1-2	
	"C" — U.21.c.8.3.	
	"D" — U.21.c.6-5	
	U.20.b.9-3.	
January 2nd to 5th	Wagon Lines march from CROMBEKE area and were	
Jan 6th.	established near ELVERDINGHE. B.7.a. Sheet 28 N.W. 1/20,000	
7th	Nothing to report. Enemy very quiet.	
8th	Batteries registered points for minor operation.	
	Nothing to report.	
	1.15 S.A. Layer No 1. Cannon Mt. A1- 4.45 am.	
	Attempt to take TURENNE Crossing was unsuccessful	
	S.O.S. case replied to A1-4.42pm, Crews firing A1- 5.30pm.	
Jan 9th to 15th 1918	Nothing to report.	
Jan 16th to 21st.	Nothing but harassing fire on enemy tracks and	
	duty pts etc. in O.36.C and D.	
Jan 22nd	One section from each Battery was detached and placed near	
	Envers. These sections were registering 22nd.	
Jan 23rd	Pill Box O.36.C.6.5.1 and MARSEILLE Fm P.25.C.2.2	
	Ammunition dump D/83 with relas[?] gas shell.	

Army Form C. 2118.

WAR DIARY
or
INTELLIGENCE SUMMARY.
(Erase heading not required.)

83rd Brigade R.F.A.

Hour, Date, Place	Summary of Events and Information	Remarks and references to Appendices
Jan 24/1/918.	Hostile Battery at 0.23.d. 9.1 engaged.	
Jan 25/1/918.	Enemy Trench Mortars engaged at V.1.a.0.5. Harassing fire on Tracks during enemy relief carried out. Six Rounds Gas Shell in 0.36.b.5.1 and 0.55.b.4.3.	
Jan 26/1/918.	Bombardment by D/83 with Rehef Shell. S.O.S. Signal reply to at 6.15 pm. Am Glass at 6.25 pm.	
Jan 27/1/918.	Enemy Huts and Cellars at 0.36.d.95.30 bombarded with gas Shell.	
Jan 28/1/918.	Chateau at 0.29.b.22.15 shelled by D/83 with Gas Shell 7.B.C. Battery's carriers not required etc.	
Jan 29/1/918.	Same programme carries out as on 28/1.	
Jan 30/1/918.	Personnel of C and D/161 relieved vectors of C and D/83 in action. Arming personnel of C and D/83 relieved by C and D/161.	
Jan 31/1/918.	C and B Batteries still in action until Bde HQ under orders of 32nd Div. Art. Casualties during month. Major R.H. Seward wounded in Action Jan 22/1/918. 2 men killed and 18 wounded during the month.	

C.R. Cruickshanks Capt for
Major R.F.A.
Commdg 83rd Bde R.F.A.

Army Form C. 2118

WAR DIARY or INTELLIGENCE SUMMARY
(Erase heading not required.)

83 Brigade RFA   Vol 31

Place	Date	Hour	Summary of Events and Information	Remarks and references to Appendices
	1/2/18		A & B Batteries were relieved by Batteries of 11th AFA Bde in action. The personnel being withdrawn to wagon lines. C & D Batteries moved to HAMHOEK Area. F18d Sh 27. HdQrs relieved by 161 Bde RFA (in action).	
HAMHOEK	2/2/18		Head Quarters and A & B Batteries moved to HAMHOEK area F18d Sheet 27	
	3/2/18 to 9/2/18		Nothing to report	
	10/2/18		Batteries left HAMHOEK Area and entrained at PROVEN en route for NOYON. A,B & C Batteries being billeted at PORQUERICOURT. D Battery billets were at VAUCHELLES	
	11/2/18		HdQrs entrained at PROVEN for NOYON & were billeted in PORQUERICOURT	
PORQUERI-COURT	12/2/18 to 14/2/18		PORQUERICOURT — Nothing to report.	
GUISCARD	15/2/18		Brigade moved to GUISCARD Area — Billets as follow A Battery — NEUVILLE EN BEINE B & C Batteries — BEINE D Battery HQ — GUISCARD	
	16/2/18		Nothing to report.	
	17/2/18		50 men per Battery under orders of 14 DA preparing Reserve Positions for Battues Zone – 2nd line of Defence E. of CLASTRES.	
	18/2/18 to 30/2/18		Nothing to report.	

WAR DIARY
or
INTELLIGENCE SUMMARY

(Erase heading not required.)

Army Form C. 2118

Instructions regarding War Diaries and Intelligence Summaries are contained in F.S. Regs., Part II. and the Staff Manual respectively. Title Pages will be prepared in manuscript.

Place	Date	Hour	Summary of Events and Information	Remarks and references to Appendices
	21/3/18		The Brigade marched from GUISCARD to FLAVY-LE-MARTEL area. Guns moved into positions for defence of Battle Zone. B. in LAST RES.	
	22/3/18 to 26/3/18		Nothing to Report.	
	27/3/18		Advance Parties took over from Batteries of 169 Bde in action.	66 CM
	28/3/18		Batteries completed relief & Hd Qrs took over from Hd Qrs of 169 Bde at CAPONNE FARM & moved to new HQ Qrs at N3 c-80-90 approx. Positions of Batteries were as follows:- A/83. H 35 b 14·77 B/83 H 35 b 48·08 C/83 H 28 a 25·80 D/83 N 10 d 80·80	66 SM

C.R. Ouichants
Lt. Col. Commanding 83 Bde RFA

for Lt. Col. Commanding 83 Bde RFA

18th Div.

WAR DIARY

Headquarters,

83rd BRIGADE, R.F.A.

M A R C H

1 9 1 8

Army Form C. 2118.

WAR DIARY
or
INTELLIGENCE SUMMARY.
(Erase heading not required.)

83rd Brigade R.F.A. Vol 32

Place	Date	Hour	Summary of Events and Information	Remarks and references to Appendices
	1.3.18		Brigade H.Q. and Batteries in action under III Corps	#4"N/3 to Thurs 66 E N/W
	2.3.18		nothing to report	
	3.3.18		Quiet day. Harassing fire carried out during night.	
H. 4.3.18/5				
	9.3.18		Snipers & harassing fire carried out.	
	10.3.18		Barrage fire put down on batteries in support of raid carried out by 14/15 D.W.	
	11.3.18		Snipers throughout the day. Harassing fire on Enemies support line.	
	12.3.18		— do —	
K 20.3.18				
	21.3.18		At 4.30 am when Batteries were carrying out harassing fire on enemy Front and Support lines, the enemy opened on the offensive with a tremendous bombardment using all calibres including gas shells on B[de] H.Q. and all Battery positions and main lines of communications. The bombardment was intense up to about 9.30 am when it slackened. Later the enemy put down another barrage moving Westwards soon after the enemy were upon the forward Battery positions	

Army Form C. 2118.

83rd Brigade R.F.A

WAR DIARY
~~INTELLIGENCE~~ SUMMARY.
(Erase heading not required.)

Place	Date	Hour	Summary of Events and Information	Remarks and references to Appendices
	22.3.18		getting close to the guns before being observed owing to the prevailing mist. All four guns were put out of action by shell[?] fire away the breech blocks. The detachments retired to their rear guns under cover of rifles inflicting severe casualties to the enemy in his advance. All guns were manned without delay and the enemy fired on, in many cases at very close range. The rear guns of B/83 and C/83 kept firing up to 9 pm when C/83 guns gave out. D/83 gun section kept firing up to midnight, the detachments withdrawing on the retirement of the infantry. B/83 rear section guns were unknown come into action again West of OISE CANAL covering the Infantry retirement under orders of 82nd Brigade. The Brigade assembled at CAUMONT.	
	23.3.18		The Brigade marched to GRANDRU.	
	24.3.18		A/83 moved to PORQUERICOURT and came under orders of 282nd Bde. R.F.A. B, C and D Btys and Bde HQ retired [?] Batteries of 82nd Bde R.F.A	

WAR DIARY
or
INTELLIGENCE SUMMARY.
(Erase heading not required.)

Army Form C. 2118.

Place	Date	Hour	Summary of Events and Information	Remarks and references to Appendices
	25.3.18		In action near CREPIGNY, firing over 8,1 Am Q.F. and 3. 4.5" How. Batteries withdraw from CREPIGNY at 10 am am dropped into action near VARESNES, firing few shots on enemy advancing to GRANDRU.	
	26.3.18		Brigade move to position at LA POMMERAYES near CUTS. Re-enforcing the French and coming under orders of 270th Regt. (French). Rein forcing French at LA POMMERAYES	
	27.3.18		do	
	28.3.18			
	29.3.18		Batteries withdraw from action and marches to OLLIZENCOURT.	
	30.3.18		Halting to refit.	
	31.3.18		Brigade, less Am 17/83, marches to RIVECOURT.	

Army Form C. 2118.

WAR DIARY
or
INTELLIGENCE SUMMARY.
(Erase heading not required.)

Instructions regarding War Diaries and Intelligence Summaries are contained in F. S. Regs., Part II. and the Staff Manual respectively. Title pages will be prepared in manuscript.

Place	Date	Hour	Summary of Events and Information	Remarks and references to Appendices
	13/4/18		Casualties during last month (MARCH).	
			2nd Lieut. D. Capperbald wounded. 6-3-18	
			Major E. Keyes M.C. wounded - believed a prisoner 21/3/18	
			Major R. H. Farrer. Prisoner — " —	
			Major H.D. MacPherson. Wounded — " —	
			2/Lt. R.J. Trevor. Wounded & missing — " —	
			2/Lt. G. Treadon. Missing — " —	
			2/Lt. J. Wood " — " —	
			2/Lt. F.E.H. Truman Killed in action — " —	
			2/Lt. E.C.H. Stephenson — " — " —	
			2/Lt. A. Brown Wounded & missing — " —	
			2/Lt. F.L. Nutter Missing — " —	
			2/Lt. R.D. Patterson Missing — " —	
			D.R.s. 9 Killed	
			30 wounded to hospital	
			7 — " — & missing	
			64 missing	

C.W.R. Cruikshank
Capt 18TR
for Lt. Col Comdg 18 & 7TR
7TR

18th Div.

Headquarters,

83rd BRIGADE, R.F.A.

A P R I L

1 9 1 8

Army Form C. 2118.

WAR DIARY
INTELLIGENCE SUMMARY

(Erase heading not required.)

87th Brigade RFA

YA33

Place	Date	Hour	Summary of Events and Information	Remarks and references to Appendices
	Apr 1st 1918		Brigade marched from RIVECOURT to VAUX sur CAMBRONNE	
	2nd 1918		VAUX sur CAMBRONNE to HAUD MAU1883	
	3rd 1918		HAUD DIVISIERS to FRANCASTEL	
	4th 1918		FRANCASTEL to MOYENCOURT	
	Apr 5th to		Refitting of Units and Guns etc was carried out.	
	Apr 8th 1918		Brigade marched from MOYENCOURT to MORVILLERS or 6p85.	
	Apr 9th 1918		Brigade halted at MORVILLERS.	
	Apr 10th 1918		The Brigade marched from MORVILLERS to WARLUS.	
	Apr 11th 1918		The Brigade marched from WARLUS to LIER COURT DUNCY	
	Apr 12th to Apr 15th		Refitting of Brigade proceeded with during stay sur LIERCOURT	
	Apr 15th		Brigade marched from DUNCY - LIERCOURT to RITERY - FOUILENS	
	Apr 16th		A.B.&D Batteries took over Sectors Sp 104, 3p 5 and 575 Bdys respectively Shew Bde HQ took over from 458 Bde HQ at Tp 7.6. Brigade now covering AUDIGNY Line.	[62]
	Apr 17th		Nothing to report	
	Apr 18th			

WAR DIARY or INTELLIGENCE SUMMARY.

Army Form C. 2118.

83rd Brigade R.F.A.

Place	Date	Hour	Summary of Events and Information	Remarks and references to Appendices
	Apl 19/5		Brigade in Corps moved to Corps in N3342c	See
	Apl 20/5 to Apl 22nd		Nothing to report	62
	Apl 23rd		Brigade with orders to move and took over from 97868 02600.3 and took over from A,B,& C Batteries took new positions respectively - 306 Brigade. B,B, & C Batteries took new positions D/83 15th New Army D/207 Batteries of 306 Brigade the Brigade was now under orders of 58th Div. Arty.	
	Apl 24/5		Enemy offensive at 3.45 a.m. with a heavy bombardment of gas shell. Batteries were in communication enemy with success B/83 engaged enemy and caused a general line to one. B/83 were ordered to withdraw owing to the enemy advance and came to rest at 019 B 24. Enemy attacks were repulsed by all batteries of the Brigade. Brigade HQ moved to T.16.d.5.8. at 6 pm.	
	Apl 25/4/18		Batteries fired bursts of fire on various targets throughout the day	
	Apl 26/4/18		Batteries fired a barrage at 5.15 am in support of a stack by the French Moroccan Div. and the 53rd Inf. Bde. Enemy attacks during times throughout the day and were repulsed or took prisoner. P.T.O	

Army Form C. 2118.

WAR DIARY
INTELLIGENCE SUMMARY
(Erase heading not required.)

53rd Brigade R.F.A.

Place	Date	Hour	Summary of Events and Information	Remarks and references to Appendices
	Apr 26th (Cont.)		Batteries fired in response to S.O.S. signals at 6.10 p.m. and 7 p.m. Targets were enemy trenches throughout the day.	
	Apr 27th		Enemy more quiet. Batteries carried out registration.	
	Apr 28th		Batteries continue to harass lines.	
	Apr 29th		Brigade withdrew from the line and moved to BETTENCOURT St Ouen	
	Apr 30/4/18		Brigade present camped at T in BETTENCOURT St Ouen. Casualties for Month — 2 Lieut F.S. Mitchell wounded 24/4/18. 2 other Ranks killed, 18 wounded.	

Rob. Cruikshank Capt
Lieut Col R.F.A.
Commdg 53rd Brigade R.F.A.

Army Form C. 2118.

WAR DIARY
INTELLIGENCE SUMMARY
(Erase heading not required.)

83rd Brigade RFA
Vol 34

Place	Date	Hour	Summary of Events and Information	Remarks and references to Appendices
	May 1st 1918		The Brigade in training area at BETTENCOURT ST OUEN	
	May 2nd 3rd 4th		Training carries out in above area	
	May 5/5/18		The Brigade marches from BETTENCOURT ST OUEN to BELLENCOURT	show
	May 6/5/18		Brigade took over from 313 Australian FA Brigade at DIGNATT	62"
			A.B. C and D Batteries relieved no 13, 14, 15 and 151st Batteries in action	
			with LOVIGNALLE Group under orders of 2nd Australian Div. Arty.	
	May 7/5/1916		Night harassing fire carried out.	
			18½ Div Arty took over from our Army Div. Arty and Brigade then	
			under orders of 18 B.D.	
	May 8/5/1918		Harassing fire and Support "Arrivee" at Ruyott Wep Wer Sap	
	May 9/5 1918		do	
	May 10/5 1918		do	
	May 11/5/18		do	
	May 12/5/18		do	
	May 13/5/1918		No night firing carried out to assist 3F Infantry relief.	

Army Form C. 2118.

WAR DIARY
or
INTELLIGENCE SUMMARY.
(Erase heading not required.)

83 Bde Brigade R.F.A

Instructions regarding War Diaries and Intelligence Summaries are contained in F. S. Regs., Part II. and the Staff Manual respectively. Title pages will be prepared in manscript.

Place	Date	Hour	Summary of Events and Information	Remarks and references to Appendices
	May 14/15 1918		Harassing fire carried out throughout night and received from our periphery guns	
	May 15/16 1918		Do	
	May 16/17 1918		At 2 am A.106 was carried out by our infantry on front from E.4.a.0.5.5 to E.5.a.5.0. Dd Battery fired down a barrage in support of this raid which lasted 35 minutes.	
	May 18/19/18		Night firing for harass on & hostile area activity	
	May 20 1918		At corps conference Operation No 2 Km engage at 3.10am	
	May 20-21/18		Enemy by day not carrying out any night. Engaged at the Brigade was relieved on the line by 236 Bde R.F.A.	
			Bde H.Q. B & C Batteries with D Battery and D Battery with	
			6 Gun inclusive to engage line at BIENCOURT and toe enemy	
			of H from same Brigade. A/63 took over from A/236 their Narrow in the line was over	
			by 3PM OC.	
	May 25 1918		Nothing to report. Casualties for month 3 ORs Wounded	

LT. R. Cruickshank Capt.
LT.-COL., R.F.A.
COMDG. 83rd BRIGADE, R.F.A.

B/1/16
Army Form C. 2118.
Vol 35
B Bde Bangre R.H.A.

WAR DIARY
or
INTELLIGENCE SUMMARY.
(Erase heading not required.)

Instructions regarding War Diaries and Intelligence Summaries are contained in F.S. Regs., Part II. and the Staff Manual respectively. Title pages will be prepared in manuscript.

Place	Date	Hour	Summary of Events and Information	Remarks and references to Appendices
	June 12th		Brigade met with B, C and D Batteries in action near HENENCOURT under Brig Genl A/63	
	June 13th		Battries in Coy'd posns camod at Treway	
	June 14th		Brigade HQ with B, C and D Batteries took over in the line the 108th Brigde RFA HQ and with D/108 and "O" Battery RHA forward left grp 14th Divl Arty. Covering the 55th Infantry Brigade. Grps B & O on V.Sec C-3. IV Corps preparation war area carrd out during the night. No 1.	RFA HQ SENLIS 3 guns
	June 15th		D/153 relieves D/108 in C. Bn and came under Bde R Left Grp. N. Battery RHA relieves "O" Battery. R.H.A. Bns came under Bde R Right grp. Supplied by day out of action. Fire flown by night. Enemy trenches and communications. Nothing to report. Usual harassing fire.	Enemy Battery activity Normal
	June 16th		do	14/20th hussars kt Beauga
	17th		do	
	18th			
	19th			B/VII relieves "N" 13th RHA
	20th			
	21st		Some Reply fire on both sides. 55th Inf Bde relief 35th Inf Bde carried out by 1st Army 18th DA	

Army Form C. 2118.

WAR DIARY
INTELLIGENCE SUMMARY.

(Erase heading not required.)

83rd Brigade R.F.A.

Place	Date	Hour	Summary of Events and Information	Remarks and references to Appendices
	June 22nd		Usual sniping by day and ev. Harassing fire by night	
	June 23rd		Hostile batteries were less active.	
	24th		Hostile snipers and harassing fire	
	25th		do	
	26th		do	
	27th		do	
	28th		do	
	29th		do	
	June 30/18		Left Group Batteries supported an attack by the 54th Infantry Brigade on enemy front line system from M.18.d.1.7 to M.13.d.5.0. Zero hour was 9.35 pm. All objectives were taken and evacuated by 12.30 am 1-7-18.	
			Casualties during June 3 O.Rs. wounded	

A.R. Cruikshank Carter
LT.-COL., R.F.A.
COMDG. 83rd BRIGADE, R.F.A.

Army Form C. 2118.

WAR DIARY
INTELLIGENCE SUMMARY.
(Erase heading not required.)

VR 36
83rd Brigade   R.4/17

Place	Date	Hour	Summary of Events and Information	Remarks and references to Appendices
	July 1st		Brigade in action near SENKIS and known as Left Group 18th Divisional Artillery. Enemy made a counter attack on our front but were beaten off. Battalion fired on enemy preparation as per 18th Divl. Arty. Orders No./33. Counter preparation fire at 9 pm and 2 am. Enemy put down enemy barrage. Attacks following were repulsed.	
	July 2nd		Enemy put down a heavy barrage and artillery fire on troops & batteries to the Rt. Front Line.	
	July 3rd		Harassing fire on enemy tracks etc. carried out. L/S Kings Shales at request of Infantry (555 Infantry Brigade) and harassing fire carried out.	
	July 4th		At 3.10 am 18th Bde. OP No.135 carried out in support of an attack by Australian troops on the River. Harassing fire also carried out on enemy lines of communication etc. Concentration burst of fire during night. Usual harassing the enemy fire carried out. Gas projectiles were discharged in our front.	
	July 5th July 6th to July 11th		Nothing but harassing fire carried out.	
	July 12th		142nd Inft. Bde retuned 55½ Inf Bde and were covered by an usual harassing programme.	

Army Form C. 2118.

WAR DIARY
or
INTELLIGENCE SUMMARY.
(Erase heading not required.)

8 Bde Bde R.F.A.

Place	Date	Hour	Summary of Events and Information	Remarks and references to Appendices
	July 13th		47th Divl. Arty relieve 18th Divl. Arty. H.Q. 8th Bde R.F.A. Brigade was under orders of 47th Divl. Arty and remained so Left Group were Covering force carried out.	
	July 14th		The Brigade who relieved in the line by 230th Brigade R.F.A. and withdrew to Bivouac area at CONTAY.	
	July 15th		The Brigade marched from CONTAY to ARGOEUVES (Somme).	
	July 16th		The Brigade in now at ARGOEUVES. Training commenced.	
	July 17th		Training St Jeanne Armes Lel.	
	& July 23rd	4		
	July 24th		Brigade Horse Show held.	
	July 25th		Training carried out in Brigade.	
	July 27th		Training carrying on.	
	July 31st		Training carry on: The Brigade is under orders proceed to forward area. Casualties during month. 2 O.Rs. wounded.	

C.A. Cruickshank Capt
for Major R.F.A.
Commdg. 8th Bde R.F.A.

18th DIVISION
ARTILLERY

83rd BRIGADE

ROYAL FIELD ARTILLERY

AUGUST 1918

WAR DIARY
or
INTELLIGENCE SUMMARY.
(Erase heading not required.)

Army Form C. 2118.

63rd Brigade R.F.A.

VR 37

Place	Date	Hour	Summary of Events and Information	Remarks and references to Appendices
Field	1/8/18		Brigade commanded by Major C.A. Drummond R.F.A.	
			The Brigade marched from ARGOEUVES (Rear Area) and took over Wagon Lines	Sheet
			from 14th Australian F.A. Brigade near FRECHENCOURT.	62d
			The positions for Battery were taken over as follows A/83 J5a.3-3 B/83 J5a.5.0	(Amiens)
			C/83 J10a.77-70. D/83 J.5. a.00-37.	
	2/8/18		Remaining sections of Batteries moved into action as above	
			Bde H.Q. moved from wagon Lines area took over from 14th A.F.A.Bde	
			in the line at T1c 60-65.	
			Harassing fire carried out by day and night on enemy approaches &	
Aug 3rd to 5th			nothing but desultory shelling on both sides.	
Aug	6th.		Enemy attacks and periodic on front Trenches but was beaten	
			back by a Counter attack by 54th Bde.	
			Heavy harassing fire by night	
Aug	7th		Enemy attacked on front again several times during the	
			day but was beaten off on each occasion. Batteries never	
			to forward positions as follows A/83 + B/83 in J.5.b. C/83 D/83 in J5.c	

Army Form C. 2118.

83rd Bde. RFA

WAR DIARY
or
INTELLIGENCE SUMMARY.
(Erase heading not required.)

Place	Date	Hour	Summary of Events and Information	Remarks and references to Appendices
MERICOURT L'ABBÉ	Aug 8th		The Division attacked at 4.20 a.m. moving very rapidly. The Brigade fired a creeping barrage on South West limit of MORLANCOURT. A and B Batteries suffered severe casualties from mustard gas. At 11 a.m. news received from F.O.O. that all objectives had been gained except on extreme left. The enemy counter-attacked from MORLANCOURT at 4.30 p.m. and succeeded in pushing the line back a little. Casualties in the Brigade heavy. All guns 6 officers 40 OR. Orders received to reconnoitre for positions on S.J. BRAY-CORBIE road. These orders cancelled later.	
	Aug 9	5.30 p.m.	attacked MORLANCOURT and high ground N and E of the village. Attack which resulted in very little opposition and sent forward targets for artillery. Reconnoitred positions near VILLE SUR ANCRE.	

Army Form C. 2118.

II

83 Bde R.F.A.

WAR DIARY
or
INTELLIGENCE SUMMARY.
(Erase heading not required.)

Place	Date	Hour	Summary of Events and Information	Remarks and references to Appendices
MERICOURT L'ABBE	May 16		Received orders to reconnoitre and occupy positions in valley South of MORLANCOURT. The reconnaissance was completed and batteries were just moving when the orders were cancelled and Brigade was ordered to North of MORLANCOURT. Batteries had 5 pm a creeping barrage of ½ hour before moving to support an attack on the high ground N.W. of Bois DE TAILLES. Batteries moved off at 7.30 p.m. A, B and C on a ridge above (Note) N. of MORLANCOURT (K.1 central) and D in valley behind them. H.Q. to K.7.c.9.7.	
MORLANCOURT	May 17		Was very heavy hostile shelling on which front, to attack and how. Answered by slow fire on SOS lines. Moved B Battery slightly to right as it was too close to C. Hostile artillery active all night. 8" hows shelled MORLANCOURT continuously. All valleys gassed.	

D. D. & L., London, E.C. WL W507/M1367 350,000 1/17 Sch. 52a Forms C/2118/14
(A5833)

Army Form C. 2118.

IV
83 Bde R.F.A.

WAR DIARY
or
INTELLIGENCE SUMMARY.
(Erase heading not required.)

Instructions regarding War Diaries and Intelligence Summaries are contained in F. S. Regs., Part II. and the Staff Manual respectively. Title pages will be prepared in manuscript.

Place	Date	Hour	Summary of Events and Information	Remarks and references to Appendices
MORLANCOURT	Aug 12		Quiet day except for intermittent shelling of Batty areas. In evening the Bde was ordered under 82nd Bde and called "THORPE'S" Group. F.A. landing at night MARETTE WOOD	
	Aug 13	4.55 a.m.	Attacked. Objective - high ground N. of BOIS DE TAILLES. Attack failed. Enemy counterattacked up valley from BRAY and forced Infantry back to original line. Artillery on our right did not assist in the bombardment where have been stopped. There was very little barrage on the valley where the counterattack was obviously to be expected. Heavy shellfire being placed on the left. Hostile artillery & trench mortars very active all night.	
"	Aug 14		MORLANCOURT and neighbouring roads shelled all day. B. Battery 3 casualties carrying up ammunition.	
"	Aug 15		MORLANCOURT again heavily shelled. Day quiet otherwise. Hostile artillery still very active. All batteries & likely battery positions shelled.	
"	Aug 16			

Army Form C. 2118.

WAR DIARY
or
INTELLIGENCE SUMMARY.
(Erase heading not required.)

Instructions regarding War Diaries and Intelligence Summaries are contained in F. S. Regs., Part II. and the Staff Manual respectively. Title pages will be prepared in manuscript.

Place	Date	Hour	Summary of Events and Information	Remarks and references to Appendices
MORLANCOURT	Aug 17		Started a tactical O.P. on ridge N. part of AVRES where all round about MEAULTE can be watched. Day quiet, but much movement behind enemy line is evident.	
"	Aug 18	4 a.m.	Enemy artillery very active all night, and our batteries in counter preparation. No fr. half an hour in two several movement by daylight. H.P. in the day. There is too much movement to view. New found captured to view.	
"	Aug 19	Day	Enemy except for some huts shelling of MORLANCOURT and neighbourhood. Do Do	
"	Aug 20			
"	Aug 21	3 a.m.	heavy burst jam & the shelling in all valley & tanks. Gas & heavy maps. seems to attack on high ground between MEAULTE and BRAY.	

WAR DIARY or INTELLIGENCE SUMMARY

Army Form C. 2118.

Place	Date	Hour	Summary of Events and Information	Remarks and references to Appendices
MORLANCOURT	Aug 22.		At 4.45 a.m. the high ground east of the ALBERT-BRAY road was attacked and taken. The Brigade fired a creeping and protective barrage until 7.5 a.m. and then ceased firing, to allow cavalry & whippet tanks to pass through and exploit the success. The Brigade then remained "in observation" in their position to deal with hostile counter attacks. The success was exceptionally hot and almost midday. Some commotion from the batteries into position. Camps for forward movement & ammunition dumps of C Batteries was put about 100 rounds were fired to it fire to the camouflage that the Brigade were to proceed into a. 6.7 p.m. orders were received that the Brigade were called "Herveway" & Army Rock Centre behind Ransom and Kennaway and called "Herveway" jump	
	Aug 23.		At 10 a.m. "Herveway front" was again spoken of. The day passed quickly. Batteries remained in position into teams, were rung to move, but at night, at 11.30 p.m. orders were received to reconnoitre and occupy new forward position near MEAULTE.	
	Aug 24		Batteries moved off at 3 a.m. (at 1 a.m. the Infantry took DECOURT DECORDEL and the high ground south of the village.)	

Army Form C. 2118.

WAR DIARY
or
INTELLIGENCE SUMMARY.
(Erase heading not required.)

Instructions regarding War Diaries and Intelligence Summaries are contained in F.S. Regs., Part II. and the Staff Manual respectively. Title pages will be prepared in manuscript.

Place	Date	Hour	Summary of Events and Information	Remarks and references to Appendices
HORLANCOURT	Aug 24		The Brigade moved the Battn. to VILLE SUR ANCRE – MEAULTE road by the MORLANCOURT–MEAULTE road to a position 'B' approx. between MORLANCOURT and the R. ANCRE in a small valley running N. & S. between MORLANCOURT and the R. ANCRE. Here they arrived but were in position near to and east of MEAULTE coming into action at dawn under heavy H.E. fire when Brigade comd. no casualties. The fire was further without the guns on the VILLE – MEAULTE road. H.Q. was established in a road on the ridge South of MEAULTE. About 4 a.m. the enemy commenced attacks on the infantry by German 'minenwerfer' fire & heavy thousands of 77 mm shells which fell mainly into the town. A heavy shelling of MEAULTE and the valley South & S.E. of it. Very heavy shelling of MEAULTE all morning, making observation difficult. Heavy & 77 mm periods all morning, making observation difficult.	
MEAULTE	Aug 25		Attacked at 2.30 a.m. & there was no resistance. Reported town held. The enemy having withdrawn during the night. At 10.30 a.m. orders received to be ready to move at short notice. Meanwhile the Brigade was already prepared. The Brigade advanced under Cdr's direct orders to the usual separate Field under to report to in their usual manner. At 9.30 p.m. orders received to march further to regain 18 Division. The march was during the night which was subject to a heavy bombardment.	

D. D. & L., London, E.C.
Wt W.1771/M2931 750,000 5/17 Sch. 52 Forms/C2118/14
(A8004)

WAR DIARY or INTELLIGENCE SUMMARY

Army Form C. 2118.

Place	Date	Hour	Summary of Events and Information	Remarks and references to Appendices
MEAULTE	Aug 25		Distance of 1000 yards when they had to bivouac for the night in the open fields without cover of any sort.	
ALBERT	Aug 26		at midday received orders to report to 18 D.A. at RECOURT. Château into B.H.Q. proceeded. Recd. orders to relieve Fusiliers on far forward toward MONTAUBAN on point. H.Q. to be near Farm R.34.b.53. Bdy Bde on FRICOURT-CONTALMAISON road. Batteries occupied positions about dusk in places - A on western side of HAPPY VALLEY between FRICOURT WH & J. RAILWAY COPSE. B N-W corner of HAMETZ C went S.A. D on opposite side of valley in front of Pt C. H.Q. in Old Trench near WILLOW PATCH	
FRICOURT	Aug 27	10 am	verbal orders received to move forward "Y" division "Hunts". Position recommended to A & C North of MONTAUBAN and for B & D ends of Willow K.P. in old trench between MONTAUBAN and HAMETZ.	

WAR DIARY or INTELLIGENCE SUMMARY

Army Form C. 2118.

Place	Date	Hour	Summary of Events and Information	Remarks and references to Appendices
FRICOURT	Aug 27		Reconnaissance into [wood?] lit by heavy fire from [?] of TRONES WOOD & M.G. fire from close range N.E. B. 1 Section of C Battery pushed forward to BERNAFAY WOOD. The situation does not appear to favour of Retaliation [attempt?] [?]. At 2 pm glasses a slow barrage [?] site of [?] to SE, 29 & of TRONES WOOD. thin [?] [?] [?] [?] about [?] pm. CPRA cannot to say that [?] [?] [?] [?] [?] as their own positions had to be [?] for his own advance — [?] last movement B and D at [?] moved to their [?] positions for the night. [?] Battery.	
MONTAUBAN	Aug 28		H.Q. was moved nearer Bgd Rele into hut in CATERPILLAR WOOD. Interviews until closing of Battery positions & H.Q. [?] [?] day.	

Army Form C. 2118.

WAR DIARY
or
INTELLIGENCE SUMMARY.
(Erase heading not required.)

Instructions regarding War Diaries and Intelligence Summaries are contained in F.S. Regs., Part II. and the Staff Manual respectively. Title pages will be prepared in manuscript.

Place	Date	Hour	Summary of Events and Information	Remarks and references to Appendices
MONTAUBAN	Aug 29	5 a.m.	attacked TRONES WOOD 5 a.m. Enemy had retreated during night. Brigade moved out to positions B and D behind LEUZ WOOD A and C between Trones & GUILLEMONT near TRONES WOOD in liaison with 5th Inf Bde. Heavy hostile shelling all day of GUILLEMONT and roads Batteries engaged many targets, attempting to hamper transport being our - camp ammunition on roads east of COMBLES.	
GUILLEMONT	Aug 30		Attacked at 5 a.m. Attack was somewhat onning to left battalion being held up by M.G. fire and 12 Divn on our right were not keeping up in line. Very heavy opposition met from FREGICOURT.	
	Aug 31		A quieter day. Hostile shelling of roads battery & support areas from Mhatle.	

D. D. & L., London, E.C. (A8604) Wt W.1771/M2031 750,000 5/17 **Sch. 52** Forms/C2118/14

Army Form C. 2118.

WAR DIARY
or
INTELLIGENCE SUMMARY

83rd Bn Engineers RotH

(Erase heading not required.)

Place	Date	Hour	Summary of Events and Information	Remarks and references to Appendices
			Casualties for August	
			Capt L.N. Inyrville } To Hospital	
			Capt F.J. Hopkins } Wounded Gas 1.8.18	
			Lieut J.G. Doney }	
			2/Lt R.D. Barclay }	
			2/Lt W.H. Currie }	
			2/Lt W Westcott } To Hospital Wounded Gas 9-8-18	
			2/Lt R.E. Walker }	
			Lt. E. Allen. To Hospital Wounded 14-9-18.	
			2/Lt Bn Bertram To Hospital Wounded 30.9.18	
			103 Other Ranks evacuated wounded.	

T.W.Mummery
Major R.E.
Comdg 83 Bn Bde R.E.H

WAR DIARY
INTELLIGENCE SUMMARY.
(Erase heading not required.)

Army Form C. 2118.

HEADQUARTERS 88th BRIGADE R.F.A.
No. G.1576
Date 3/9/16

Vol 39 B 49

Place	Date	Hour	Summary of Events and Information	Remarks and references to Appendices
	Sept 1st 1916	5 am	Brigade in action near KEUX MILL. Supported an attack by battalion on FREGICOURT. Later swinging back to MORVAL.	
		5 pm	Brigade main support to attack and capture of RANCOURT. Battery established near PRIEZ Fm. Battalion captured by 85th Bn Fus. at 7 pm. SAILLY and SAILLISEL. Captured as a 2nd Objective.	
			An enemy movement pursued to ST PIERRE VAAST Wood. Harassing fire carried out during the night.	
	Sept 2nd		Battalion in action north of RANCOURT. Barrage fires at 5.30 am in support of an attack on GOVERNMENT FARM. Rest of day quiet. Enemy scattered. Himself in No 2 Vauxb. Vaux Wood.	
	Sept 3rd		Orders received at 9 am to move forward quietly to position on RANCOURT — GOVERNMENT FARM Rd in support of 53rd Inf Bde. Orig. Orange position covers the attack on ST Pierre Vaast and in hip between it and VAUX Wood. Batteries were ordered to sweep ground from the entrance NURLU Rd. with batteries and roads with horsey's awaiting arrival between ST PIERRE VAAST and VAUX Wood. A and C Batteries for support between ST PIERRE VAAST SW of the Rd. B and D Batteries for the tailway to ST GOVERNMENT FARM. Bde HQ established to North. Hostile Artillery continued very active on roads and battery positions.	

D.D. & L., London, E.C.
(A.10166) W(W5300/P713 750,000 2/15 Sch. 52 Forms/C.2118/16

Army Form C. 2118.

WAR DIARY
INTELLIGENCE SUMMARY
(Erase heading not required.)

62nd Brigade 7-8

Place	Date	Hour	Summary of Events and Information	Remarks and references to Appendices
Sept 4th			A Divis: Brig: Artillery Corps Dropping the Enemies arc at BRAY and enemy trenches in front, whilst workers forward over CANAL DU NORD and were relieved by 12th Division.	
	Sept 5th	5:15am	Batteries fired in support of an attack on NURLU. this attack was unsuccessful, the infantry being held up by strong hostile M.G. fire. The Brigade came under sharp shell fire and M.G. fire. 63rd Bde R.F.A. together with Bde H.Q. and cookers came up from DEM St PL, together forming a group under orders of one R.G. Longton Cmd. 250 [illegible] 62nd H.Q., who took Bde Brigade to advance across the Canal in the evening. It was not however possible, the enemy still having direct observation over the crossing. NURLU was again attacked at 7pm. Hostile Artillery very active during the night; being for shelling of BUITTON [?] positions and Bde HQ.	
Sept 6th			C/A Btty fired 1 Section S.D. Battery moved across Canal at Dawn and fired a burst at 6am in support of attack on NURLU. This place was taken with slight opposition. Bdes and Brig: very quiet. Rest of Day very quiet. The Remainder of the Brigade moved up East of Sty Rey Canal and occupied Position Near BIGNUL Copse. This under was to be RFA Bn R.F.A. (Enemy had been retired west and of ways of Battalion. Brigade withdrew from the line and marched to Rest Area at MONTAUBAN.	
Sept 7th				

WAR DIARY
INTELLIGENCE SUMMARY

Army Form C. 2118.

53rd Bgde [?]

Place	Date	Hour	Summary of Events and Information	Remarks and references to Appendices
Sept 11th Sept 11th Sept 11th			The Brigade remained in Reserve at MONTAUBAN. The Brigade moves up from MONTAUBAN to ERVAL BANK in T.O R 70 HE Valley. Staff in IIIrd Corps Reserve.	See Sheet No. 57A No. 1A
Sept 11th Sept 17th Sept 17th			IIIrd Corps Reserve. Bde went into action taking up position as follows: D/85 T.9 a u.8 A/85 T.9 q Central. B/85 T.9 b 4.2 C/85 T.9 a u.8. Fore HQ T9a v.8 D/85 T9 a 8.7 Company 63rd Sgt Bde.	
	Sept 18th	5.20am 5 pm	Batteries fired a barrage in support of attack by 63rd Inf Bn. Objectives were taken and Boyne moved up into position in F.20 a 7.5 A barrage was fired in support of an attack by 55th Inf Bde. Barrage fire was carried out taking ordinary quiet during night. Barrage fire from 11am to 1pm in support of an attack	
	Sept 19th		by 55th Inf Bde. During the afternoon hostile Batteries were very active, and Aeroplanes N.F. calls amounts. A Creeping Barrage was fired at 2.30pm. S.O.S. call at 7.25pm answered, keeping fire on X.7 west 2 Green was carried on during the night. Harassing fire and Counter Preparation was carried out during the Sept 20th	

WAR DIARY
INTELLIGENCE SUMMARY

Army Form C. 2118.

(Erase heading not required.)

53rd Brigade R.F.A.

Place	Date	Hour	Summary of Events and Information	Remarks and references to Appendices
	Sept 21.	5.40pm	Batteries fired Barrage in support of an attack by 54th Inf Bde. All objectives were gained. Hostile Battries [Batteries] were quiet at 1st, but became active later also engaged in response to aeroplane calls. Harassing fire carried on during day and night.	
	Sept 22. Sept 23.		— do —	
	Sept 24.		Barrages were fired at 3am and 5am. Retaliation Barrage was RUDIMONT Fm also fired. At 11.30am in response to SOS call by 12th Durham Battn E.P. No 2 Fr 3 to End. Harassing fire carried on during night.	
	Sept 25.		SOS Call answered at 10am. 10h Antitanks Bns relieved Bns here in the line and the Battries and 54 retained their line. The Brigade again moved into the line and took over from 3 here Bde R.F.A. Covering 54th Inf Bde. Positions :- Bde Hq M28a9.3. A/53 W28b5.0; B/53 M29.6.7. c/53 M29a55. Roaline :- Bde Hq E5a9.8 D/53 E5a9.8.	
	Sept 26.		Harassing fire carried on. During day and night.	
	Sept 27.	5.30am	Barrage fired and Infantry gained all objectives. Harassing fire carried on. Bde moved up and took Positions as follows. Bde Hq E5d9.8. A/53 F2a11. B/53 X26b1.6 c/53 F2b27. D/53 X26a6.2	

WAR DIARY
INTELLIGENCE SUMMARY

Army Form C. 2118.

Ben Bryne

Place	Date	Hour	Summary of Events and Information	Remarks and references to Appendices
	Sept 28/18		Barrage fire for Div 18th Div. OO. 145. New positions were Reservoirs in Ft. Points S. fire carried out on VEND HUILE.	Ben Bryne Rev. G.S.O. N.E.
	Sept 29/18		Harassing fire carried out.	
	Sept 30/18	2pm	Infantry patrols pushed forward into VEND HUILE and Batteries were ordered to fire on Roads running N.E. from RICHMOND QUARRY. Enemy seen forward to positions to follow and opened 5.4 h Infpose. Bde HQ. F9a 5-7. A/83 F4c 9.5. B/83 F10a 9.8. C/83. F4 c 8.6. D/83. F4c 30. F4c 8.5.	
			Battle casualties during month.	
			Lt. G.W. Kenny & Lt Doyle Wounded 18.9.18. Mr. W. Whitsitt 1 to hospital. 2 ORs Killed. 13 - Wounded.	Capt. Cruickshank R.F.A Lieut-Col Commdg 83rd Brigade R.F.A

Army Form C. 2118.

WAR DIARY
INTELLIGENCE SUMMARY.
(Erase heading not required.)

October 1918.

93rd Brigade R.F.A.

Place	Date	Hour	Summary of Events and Information	Remarks and references to Appendices
Field	1/10/18		Brigade in action as follows:- Bde H.Q. T8 a 5.7. 17 Battery T12 g 5.	Sheet 57c N.E.
			B/63. T10 a 88. C: Battery T4 e 8.6. D: Battery T4 & 8.0.	
			Enemy Artillery quiet. Our Batteries engaged hostile Batteries	
			13½ Corps relieves 3rd Corps in the Line and Brigade comes 149 Bde Infantry	
			Brigade 50th Division.	
	2/10/18		Serving the Line. Quiet day.	
	3/10/18		Batteries fired Barrage in accordance with 18½ Bde B.17. Order No 146 at 6 am.	
			Standing Barrage fires at K15 C17 12 K15 T.	
			Enemy Artillery quiet. Parts of fire carried n/c during afternoon	
			on Protection Barrage Line.	
	4/10/18		Barrage fires at 6.10 am in accordance with 18½ D.A. B.M. 71.	
			Enemy Machine Guns around HARGICOURT Farm engaged with chief overcoats.	
			Enemy massing for Counter attack near front or by Batteries at 11.00 hrs	
			and 1.200 hrs. Several hostile Batteries also engaged during afternoon. Sheet	62 NW.
			New positions were reconnoitred and rectified as follows:-	
			Bde HQ B13 c4.3. A/63. B13 a 3.3. B/63. B13 b 3. C/63. B19 a 4.3. D/63 B17 a 2.7	
	5/10/18		Enemy N.E. and covering 150th Infantry Brigade. O.P. Brocarls at B15 b 8.0.	
			Enemy very active with Artillery and Enemy Aircraft dropped many bombs.	

Army Form C. 2118.

WAR DIARY
INTELLIGENCE SUMMARY.
(Erase heading not required.)

53rd Brigade R.F.A.

October 1918.

Place	Date	Hour	Summary of Events and Information	Remarks and references to Appendices
Lunes.	5/10/18.		Wagon Lines moved up, on position A.4. B/53. A.9.b.7.0. C/53. A.9.a.95.81 D/53. A.9.a.95. B1. D/53. A.9.a.6.8.	Sh.57c S.W. & Sh.57d N.W.
	6/10/18.		No movement. Enemy artillery very active.	
	7/10/18.		Enemy artillery very quiet. During afternoon and evening enemy artillery became very active round GRAND COURT.	
	8/10/18.		Barrage fire at 05.10 as per 18th Divn Order No. 147. Battery staffs were relieved at 07.45. That attack was going well - batteries went into action again in T.25.c. At 11.00 kms a large party of the enemy were seen massing E of VIKERS OUTREAUX in T.16.a and b. These were engaged and dispersed by batteries. At 3pm BHQ moved up to LA SABLONNIERE farm in B.4.a. Batteries moved up and came into action on the road running S.E. to TIGA. Forward limber lines were established in T.16.a. Enemy aircraft very active all night, bombing and firing M.G. on roads.	Sh.57c S.W. & Sh.57d S.W.

Army Form C. 2118.

WAR DIARY
INTELLIGENCE SUMMARY.
(Erase heading not required.)

Bm Brigade RFA

November 1918

Place	Date	Hour	Summary of Events and Information	Remarks and references to Appendices
France	9/10/18		Brigade moved forward to harass enemy with South African Infantry Brigade and finally occupied positions as follows. Bm HQ P17 a 59. A/B. 733 a 2.7. B/B. P27 c 10.25. C/B. P23 a 22.87. D/B. P27 c 10.75. A Barrage was arranged on the High Green between P24 Central and Q13 Central and BOUERIES Jn. but was afterwards cancelled as news was received that enemy were leaving REUMONT and TROISVILLES. At very first lines came up to the vicinity of SERAIN.	Page 599-9
	10/10/18		Quiet night. Brigade was in Divisional Reserve. At 11am orders received from 18th Divn. Arty to push forward and engage the enemy retreating E from K6 CATEAU. Brigade moved up and came into action. HQ. P12 c 5.6. A/B. P12 c 5.6. B/B. P26 7.2 C/B. P26 7.7 D/B. P26 9. Enemy the 1991/5 D.I.F. Barrage until enemy South African Bde came up R11.12 and K36 were fired on towards sunken road near Chateau at P27 a.	Page 9-1
	11/10/18		Quiet day. Infantry pushing probes forward including heavy MG fire very little Artillery fire on their areas. At 0120 enemy lorries Brigade moved up to k G P7.	
	12/10/18		Brigade moved up to V14. Enemy shelling of Battery area normal. At MARET Z & V.I.A. line formed a Barrage in support of South African Brigade whose objective was a line K112 5/5 - K17 Central - N17 d 02 - R22 6.3. Division a Left. Bn 33rd Division a Right. Barrage afterwards became a Bge. Composition will for attack the enemy fell and threw HE on Battery positions but caused a number of our 2300 Known	

WAR DIARY or INTELLIGENCE SUMMARY

Army Form C. 2118.

83rd Bde RFA

October 1918

Place	Date	Hour	Summary of Events and Information	Remarks and references to Appendices
France	13/10/18		During the forenoon Enemy artillery very active, Battery positions being shelled heavily. At 1400 hrs Batteries fired in retaliation and proceeded to wagon lines. Laid SP B=R=T=Y. Bde Hdqrs at P26.a.33.	
	14/10/18 15/10/18		Cleaning up etc. Ambulance Exercises.	
	16/10/18		Brigade moved into action evening 1918. Left Bns as follows: Bde HQ Q27a.Q1a A/83 Q2.b.3.3 B/83 Q2.b.5.5.5. C/83 Q1a.5.0. D/83 Q2a.9.5.15. Sh 57B/20000	
	17/10/18	15.30	At 15.30 hrs Creeping Barrage fired in a N.E direction in accordance with 189 S.A. Order No 149 dated 16/10/18. At 1300 Enemy Counter attacked and after heavy fighting our infantry the line of Railway E of LE CATEAU. 200 yds S of Shea Line at Gorse Hill.	Sh 57B/20000
	18/10/18	15.30	At 15.30 Enemy attack continued by 66 Division Infantry in conjunction with 185 S.A. Order No 150. Creeping Barrage fired night during the advance on. Ammn Expenditure 400 rounds 18pr, 75 rounds 4.5 Hvy.	
	19/10/18 20/10/18	11.00	At 11.00 hrs Barrage fires as 185 S.A. No 151 B.M. 812. Supporting IV Corps on our left in their attack. Harassing fire carried out during night on roads and approaches East of SOS Line Expenditure 300 rounds 18pr 75 rounds 4.5 How.	
	21/10/18		Enemy shelling heavier than usual. Our own and Enemy artillery remained comparatively quiet during day. EAST of SOS Line during night Enemy artillery active.	

Army Form C. 2118.

WAR DIARY
or
INTELLIGENCE SUMMARY.
(Erase heading not required.)

October 1918.   6th Brigade R.F.A.

Place	Date	Hour	Summary of Events and Information	Remarks and references to Appendices
France	22/7/18		The Brigade took over with positions as follows:— HQ. C.4.b.64 (ACQTAY) P/B. K33.d.33. B/B. K33.d.53. C/B. K35.a.9.u. D/B. K33.c.31. Harassing fire carried out on roads, railway etc during moving target. enemy forward.	Sheet 57B
	23/7/18		At 0120 hrs D/B spent five guns on another + guns of new fire in a central task. 181st D.A. Instructions 10.18 am ref. enemy Cherry Lane Sp 181st Division Attack 5.3n Infantry Brigade on Right 54L " " Left. Enemy Artillery was found to be [illeg] At 0100 hrs enemy artillery fire was [illeg] alerted from SP the Brigade out of action, Owing to casualties to officers, personnel and guns it was found impossible for the Brigade to answer SOS signals to enemy front line Brigade positions :— HQ. C.9.a. Central (CHAPEL HILL.1AS) (KEMMEL) mile. A/B. A.9.d.4.3. B/B. A.9.c.1.0. B/B. A.9.a.6.2. D/B. B.5.B.52.	Sheet 57B
	24/7/18			
	24/25/7/18		Brigade in reserve at Troop Lane to [illeg] Sps. [illeg] Ammunition and others Enemy gas Shells on N.	

WAR DIARY
INTELLIGENCE SUMMARY

Army Form C. 2118.

53rd Group R.F.A.

Place	Date	Hour	Summary of Events and Information	Remarks and references to Appendices
France	30/10/18		Brigade moved into action at 10h with probable positions Group 53rd Sig. Bde. M.G. F.29 a.w.b. 7/B. F.23 b. 22.47. B/13. F.23 a. 20.09. C/13. F.23.40.70. D/B. F.24 b. 58.95. Battery remained silent during night.	Sheet 57B
	31/10/18		53rd Infantry Brigade 5th Div. took 53rd Inf Bde in the line. Harassing fire carried out by Bdy during night. Casualties during month. 2/Lt. O.E. Stepping Killed in action 17.10.18. Capt. J.H. Harvie Wounded — 23.10.15. 2/Lt. J.P. Parr — 23.10.15. 2/Lt. S.M.S. Mason — 23.10.15. 2/Lt. A. Edmonds — 18.10.15. 2/Lt. R.M. Hutchin — 23.10.15. 3 Other Ranks Killed in Action. 3 " " Wounded.	

C.R. Cruickshank Capt.
R.A. F.39
Commanding 53rd Bde R.F.A.

Army Form C. 2118.

WAR DIARY

INTELLIGENCE SUMMARY.

(Erase heading not required.)

Instructions regarding War Diaries and Intelligence Summaries are contained in F. S. Regs., Part II. and the Staff Manual respectively. Title pages will be prepared in manuscript.

83 Brigade R.F.A.

Place	Date	Hour	Summary of Events and Information	Remarks and references to Appendices
November 1st 1918			Brigade in action covering the 53rd Infantry Brigade positions as follows Bde H.Q. F.27.d.4.1 A/83 F.23.d.22.97. B/83 F.23.d.90.09 C/83 F.23.d.40.70 D/83 F.29.b.58.95 Harassing fire carried out during day and night on roads and tracks.	
	November 2nd		Usual harassing fire carried out.	
	November 3rd		------do------ 2 Hostile Batteries situated at A.11.b.8.8 and A.18.d.1.3 were engaged by batteries of this Brigade. 83rd Brigade covered the 65th Brigade front while they were moving forward.	
	November 4th	6-15 a.m.	Barrage fired in accordance with 18th D.A.I No.6 dated 3/11/18. All objectives gained after very heavy fighting in PREUX. Batteries moved forward to positions as under H.Q. A.21.a.7.9. (PREUX) A/83 A.11.c.4.1 B/83 A.17.c.7.5 C/83 A.17.a.5.4 D/83 A.17.d.5.9. Harassing fire carried out by night on Cross Roads ,B.10.c. and B.11.b. and valley B.16.b.	
	November 5th		The Brigade moved forward to H.Q. B.7.d.5.3. A/83 B.9.d.1.6.; B/83 B.9.d.9.7. C/83 B.9.d.6.3. D/83 B.10.b.5.1 Harassing fire carried out between 11 p.m. and 1 a.m EAST of the River SAMBRE C.20.b. and 21 a., sunken road and orchard.	
	November 6th		The Brigade withdrew from the line at 6 p.m. to BOUSIES village	
	November 7th		Brigade in Corps Reserve - BOUSIES village	
	November 8th		The whole of the Brigade marched to REUMONT and billetted in this village and still in Corps Reserve	
	November 8th to 11th		In Corps Reserve	
	November 11th		Hostilities ceased	

Army Form C. 2118.

WAR DIARY
or
INTELLIGENCE SUMMARY.
(Erase heading not required.)

Instructions regarding War Diaries and Intelligence Summaries are contained in F. S. Regs., Part II. and the Staff Manual respectively. Title pages will be prepared in manuscript.

Place	Date	Hour	Summary of Events and Information	Remarks and references to Appendices
	November 11th to 30th		The whole of Brigade remained in NEUMONT and were employed in salving.	
			Battle casualties during month 1 Driver wounded 1 Gunner —	

9/12/18

C.R. Cruickshank
Major OC
Comg. 83 Bde R.F.A.

Army Form C. 2118.

WAR DIARY
or
INTELLIGENCE SUMMARY
(Erase heading not required.)

83rd BRIGADE R.F.A.

Place	Date	Hour	Summary of Events and Information	Remarks and references to Appendices
	1918			
Field	Dec 1st		The Brigade billetted in REUMONT Village. Parties from each battery carried out salvage work under orders of the 54th Inf. Bde.	
	Dec 2nd		The Brigade attended a REVIEW of the 18th Division by the Divisional Commander at SERAIN.	
	3/23		Salvage work still being carried out under the orders of the 54th and 55th Infantry Brigades.	
	5th		REUMONT visited by H.M. The King, the Brigade formed up in REUMONT Square on this occassion	
	23 to 26		A general holiday for Xmas.	
	27th to 31st		Salvage work continued as above.	
			10-1-19.	

C.H. Cruickshank
Major R.F.A.
Commanding 83rd Brigade R.F.A

Army Form C. 2118.

WAR DIARY
or
INTELLIGENCE SUMMARY.
(Erase heading not required.)

83rd Brigade R.F.A.

Vol 42

Place	Date	Hour	Summary of Events and Information	Remarks and references to Appendices
	Jany 1st		The Brigade Billetted in Reumont Village. (Holiday).	5/2/19
	2 to 16th		Salvage work carried out under orders of 54th & 55th Infy Bdes	
	17th		Salvage party under orders of 54 Infy Bde withdrawn; returned to Reumont	
	30th		Salvage party under orders of 55 — returned to Reumont	
			The following officers, men and horses were demobilised during the month :-	
			1st. Major. C.H. Atkinson M.C.	
			18th 2/Lt. H. Hughes	
			24th 2/Lt. P. Hamilton	
			27 2/Lt. F.D. Smith M.C.	
			28 2/Lt. H.C. Barnes	
			31st 2/Lt. H.O. Yammer M.C.	
			O.Rs. 95.	
			Horses 90.	

A.R. Cruickshank
Lt.Col RFA for Lt Col
Commanding 83 Brigade R.F.A.

Army Form C. 2118.

83rd Brigade R.F.A. 5/3/19

Vol 43

WAR DIARY
INTELLIGENCE SUMMARY.
(Erase heading not required.)

Instructions regarding War Diaries and Intelligence Summaries are contained in F. S. Regs., Part II. and the Staff Manual respectively. Title pages will be prepared in manuscript.

Place	Date	Hour	Summary of Events and Information	Remarks and references to Appendices
REUMONT.	Feby 1st		The Brigade Billetted in Reumont village.	
	11th		Spare Harness & Stores dumped in Soda Water Factory CAUDRY.	
	13th		Guns & Amm Wagons parked at Divnl Gun Park CAUDRY.	
			The following Officers, Men & Animals were demobilized during the Month.	
			O Rs 84	
			Animals 52	
	Feby 1st		2/Lt R.L. Manby.	
	5th		Capt. F.A.F. Slight. M.C.	
	8th		Capt. W.B. Cruickshank.	
	21st		Capt. N.O. Hutton. M.C.	
	24th		Lt. C.H. Lidstone.	

H. Hutton
Capt R.F.A. for Lt.Col.
Commanding 83rd Brigade R.F.A.

Confidential

D.A.A.G. (1)

Herewith War Diary of 83rd Bde R.F.A for the month of March 1919.

W.E. Rumbold Col
i/c R.A. Section

8.4.19.

WAR DIARY
or
INTELLIGENCE SUMMARY. 83 Brigade R.F.A.

Army Form C. 2118.

Place	Date	Hour	Summary of Events and Information	Remarks and references to Appendices
MONTIGNY	14/3/19		The Brigade moved from BEVMONT to MONTIGNY. The following Officers, men & animals were transferred during the month. Major J.D. Batt. M.C. (RAMC) 11 Offs + 134 animals to 5th Army College. Major G. Heygate DSO } to U.K. pending 140 Ors. to U.K. for Demob. 2/Lt. F.W.R. Smith-Stewart transfer to the Bart. Capt. C.E. Wolfe (RAVC) to No 9 Vet Hpl Dieppe. 70 Animals to Dieppe for Sale in U.K. 59 " " Cambrai for Sale France 104 " " Abbeville	5/4/19

Bradford
LT.-COL., R.F.A.
COMDG. 83rd BRIGADE, R.F.A.

WAR DIARY
or
INTELLIGENCE SUMMARY.

Army Form C. 2118.

Place	Date	Hour	Summary of Events and Information	Remarks and references to Appendices
Montargy	July		Brigade stationed at Montargy	
"	29/7/19		H.Q. & "A" Battery Equipment Guns to U.K	
"	29/7/19		B.C. & D. Batteries Equipment Guns to U.K.	

J.H. Weldon
Capt. R.F.
Commanding 75 Brigade R.F.A.

www.ingramcontent.com/pod-product-compliance
Lightning Source LLC
Chambersburg PA
CBHW082010220426
43670CB00014B/2596